my Life in public housing

My Life in Public Housing

CALIBER 44

iUniverse

MY LIFE IN PUBLIC HOUSING

iUniverse books may be ordered through booksellers or by contacting:

iUniverse
1663 Liberty Drive
Bloomington, IN 47403
www.iuniverse.com
1-800-Authors (1-800-288-4677)

ISBN: 978-1-5320-7770-8 (sc)
ISBN: 978-1-5320-7771-5 (e)

Print information available on the last page.

iUniverse rev. date: 06/24/2019

Introduction

This book is dedicated to all the residents of public housing. What they have to put up with other people living in their complex that cause problems for other tenants. Drugs, crime and general annoyance from other tenants and their animals. Also the neglect of the owners, of the complex, to take care of multiple problems, both with tenants and taking care of the property properly. The poor background check they do before letting in new tenants. When a tenant complains, to the owners, about a problem they either get a poor or no response to the complaints.

My Life in Public Housing

A Day to Day Account

It was a clear morning and 70 out, as the sun began to peek, over the trees, you could hear kids yelling at each other.

Then cats were running around the complex. You could hear the chickens and ducks that got out of their coop and were all over the field. Soon afterwards the skunks showed up.

As the morning progressed neighbors were arguing with each other.

As early afternoon you could see flashing lights coming down the road. It was the ambulance and EMTs scurrying around. Soon they emerged with a tenant on a gurney. The ambulance wized out of here with flashing lights and a siren going on. As things quieted down then the state police came looking for someone. Followed by the sheriff who was here to serve an eviction, on a tenant.

As the sun began, to set, you could here a mother, from the family units, swearing at her kids.

Then all was quiet, as the sun set and the darkness came. So ends a normal day at public housing. As tenants locked up, for the night. Who knows what tomorrow will bring. As a day, in public housing passes on.

When I moved in I understood I was moving into a senior unit. As it turned out the 12 so-called senior units, were occupied by 6 seniors and 6 non-seniors. Five of those non-seniors are on disability and one with no income.

Property managers come and go like flies.

Owners maintenance were scurrying around just to make a good impression, on the new manager. Then we do not see them again.

Tenants spend more time taking care of things here, then the owners do. Flower gardens, trimming bushes and trees and weeds that the mowers ignore.

Roads are full of holes, trees dying, siding damaged, sidewalks in very poor condition, rain gutters incomplete and done wrong. Rehab was done by a 3rd. Rate contractor who did an extremely poor job and incomplete work.

We have tenants, with disabilities and owners do not accommodate their needs.

Maintenance spends more time visiting, doing errands for and favoring one tenant over others, instead of doing his job.

Our senator was asked to intervene, on behalf of tenants, to help us. No results as our problems are not big enough to get him on tv.

So many tenants have been evicted for non-payment of rent. Owners do a poor background check, before letting in a tenant.

Some tenants spend their time watching other tenants. What they do, when they come and go, who comes to see them and then they spread stories, often untrue, about other tenants.

For a long time drug dealers came to supply some tenants and one tenant who resells. On weekends a line of cars coming and going for a fast 5 minute pickup of drugs, at one family unit. Those tenants were evicted.

Now the summer heat and humidity keep tenants inside. So the smokers, smoke inside, against the complex policy, of no smoking in apartments.

Maintenance finally got around to trim bushes and trees, that touch the building. But it looks more like butchering bushes and trees. But still neglecting important things that need attention here.

Maintenance man more and more has been taking one tenant to do her personal errands and shopping, in the company van. That can get him fired. But you hardly see the property manager. She was hired two months ago and already took a weeks vacation. You can not manage property, like this complex, if you do not even come here, to see what is going on.

One tenant has had so many broken windows. He blames his kids, when they come. Not likely since there are punched holes, in the walls. Front door chalked up, by the kids and markers drawn on the walls. He has cats that are not fixed.

When I moved in the rule was only two pets and only a small dog. No large dogs. In the family unit one tenant has five cats and a big dog. One tenant there has three large dogs. New tenant that just moved in has a large dog. The five cats run loose all over the complex. Rule says only inside cats.

Some tenants do not pay their rent and then go, to the valley fund and expect them to give them the money, to pay up back rent and more. A new tenant just moved into the family unit with her 2 1/2 year old daughter. Now her boyfriend's lease is up, on his apartment. So he is going to move in with her. Normally the rent would increase based on his income. But she going to claim he pays rent, to his mother, so they think because he pays rent somewhere else that him living with her, full time, will not change her rent. Just another scam, to avoid paying what she should pay. So many tenants pull things to try to get out of meeting their obligations, for living here.

They take advantage, of the system which has a major lack of oversight. I've tried to tell the owners that they need someone here at least a few hours every day. So they can see what really goes on here.

HUD pays the difference between what the tenant pays, based on their income, and the full rental price. This is our tax money that we all payed in for long years. Ones that are taking advantage have paid little tax money, because they are new, to the job market. But they sure have learned all the ways of taking advantage, of their situation and get things for free.

There's a young man who comes on Saturday, who cleans the common room and the laundry room. Also the laundry room, at the family units, where kids hang out. Just found out that he is a three time sex offender. This shows another incident, that the owners do not do a background check on people they hire.

One tenant plans to go to Florida, for the winter and keep her apartment by paying the rent. She thinks she can go for 6 months, come back for a month and then go again. My understanding is HUD's requirements are you must live in your apartment at least 6 months straight a year, to keep them paying.

A contractor came and measured the sidewalk and areas marked for changes, three months ago. But so far nothing has been done. We have had perfect weather, in long enough stretches, to redo the sidewalk; but nothing.

Holes in the road have gotten worse then ever. No sign that is going to be fixed soon. Area along road, weeds are 4 feet high, and make's this place look like a dump. No sign of mowing down these weeds. Mowers have been neglecting to weed wack by buildings and other areas.

After time again and again complaints about one tenant's mess outside his apartment and his kids junk all over the common area, nothing done about it.

A new tenant that's only been, in the family unit a few days. While she was at work the new property manager and the maintenance man walked into her apartment. The owner's own regulations say that they must give no less than a 48 hour notice for the purpose of; inspecting the apartment, making repairs, providing agreed upon services or other reasons. Now HUD's regulations says; the right to be given reasonable notice, in writing, of any nonemergency inspection or other entry into your apartment. Both persons are in violation of the owners rules and HUD's. Also this is a violation of her civil rights. This is not a prison of war camp.

This morning, early, there was a cat fight between two cats that always run loose.

One tenant whose in a wheel chair because of spinal injury, from a car accident, and can not use his legs. Fell out of his chair and broke his leg, having surgery.

At one point the owners had a tree service come and take down dead trees and problem trees. But they never had them trim other trees. Especially with branches laying against the family unit building. But today three, of the maintenance men came and tried to cut about a 6 inch diameter branch leaning on the building. Well it was like the three stooges. They put a rope on it about 3 feet from where they would cut it. Rope should have been on the end. They backed a pickup truck underneath and one guy stood up on top of the side of the bed, 4 inches wide and tried to cut with a chainsaw, over his head. As soon as a cut was made the branch pressed against the building and the chainsaw bound up, in the cut. Then, with a pole cutter, by hand to cut away wood so they could get the chainsaw out and finished cutting by hand with the pole saw. Then left and left everything laying, on the ground. They came back the next day and randomly cut branches, on several trees and never tried to actually shape trees. It looks just like they hacked away at it. They did clean up and take all the branches away.

The new property manager was arrogant and flipen, with a tenant, about her cats. Because the tenant was waiting for paperwork, from the owners, who never sent them, before they got their shots and a young female was fixed. When the property manager came around, to have papers signed, not related, to the cats. The tenant put her in her place and told her to get out of her unit. Also told her on the upcoming inspection she did not want that manager, in her unit.

A tenant in a family unit moved out. She was fed up with how this place is run and things not taken care of.

There are still tenants living here doing drugs. They had evicted several of the problem tenants and turn around and let new tenants move in that should have never been allowed here.

A new tenant, in a family unit, got written up for a ridicules reason.

There's a tenant, in a wheel chair, and he is paralyzed from the waist down. His two small kids come every other weekend. All they do is scream, mark up the sidewalk, his front door and all over the unit's walls. There is so much junk piled up at his front and back doors. He has broken multiple windows. Now he somehow broke his leg. In the hospital they arranged for him to go to rehab, in a week when a place is available. They wanted him to stay, in the hospital, because if he had another infection it could kill him. Instead he checked himself, out of the hospital and got his mother to drive him home. Then all he did was yell and swear, at his mother. She was in tears.

Now we have another resident, in a wheel chair, who every time someone has a medical problem she runs and tells them what to do. She went over and chewed that fellow out and scolded his kids. And tell him what he should have done and stayed, in the hospital. We refer to her as the resident witch doctor.

The complex rules say no washing of cars or changing oil or any kind of vehicle repairs. A vehicle has been on a jack with the left front wheel missing for at least a month. Property manager never wrote them up; but wrote up others for ridicules reasons.

Now the owners are coming around with people from React. They never told us who they are or what the inspection is for or about. They put off the sidewalk repairs because of the inspection. We have been waiting 6 years for them to repair the sidewalk.

They filled holes, in the driveway and a washed out area, with stay mat and stones racked up from the roadway. But never filled the really bad holes in the main road, at the turn, to this property. None of that will stay as loose material in a compacted hole will be gone soon.

The service mowed the lawn two days ago. Now they had them come back and remow the morning, of the inspection, to make the place look good instead of fixing things that have been needed done for years. They done all this and the inspection was a joke. The person from React only checked if doors were ok, in the unit and the toilet worked and the alert switch worked.

They checked most of the family units but only checked every other unit in the senior part. The man from React had a bad attitude. He acted like he was some kind of bigshot. He moved my table that was beside my bed so he could check the door. He knocked stuff off my table, onto the floor and left the table by the foot of my bed and never picked up what he knocked off.

Instead of this crap they need to stop the drug use here and the people that are bringing in drugs.

Well they finally came and redid the sidewalk by putting another asphalt layer over the old two layers.

One tenant half the time is drunk or high on marijuana. She wears a pain patch all the time. With that combination other tenants hear her throwing up and then she calls the ambulance. She is usually back, to her unit, in a few hours.

One tenant whose on disability and takes a lot of different medications. When some little thing happens she gets so worked up and in tears. Example; her neighbor got dish for tv and they put it about 30 feet, from the building, in the lawn. She got so worked up about having to look at it when she's outside.

After all that's been going on now we have a power outage. What more can happen.

The new tenant, in the family unit, just started a new job two weeks ago. The first week she said she did not feel good and took the day off. The second week she said the same thing and took the day off. Both times she's been seen sitting outside, with her boy friend. She keeps this up she will loose her job.

Today was another one of those days where the maintenance man only came here to take a tenant to do her personnel errands, in the company van. I see she just came back with a bag from the grocery store. He should be fired for this. But no one, from the owners, are ever here except when they have an inspection.

Already there are people driving over the new sidewalk. At that rate it will not last long.

They have been installing new dish antennas for tv. They are putting them on the ground. They will eventually take the ones, off the roof, and put them on the ground on a post. It's already making this place look like a space station.

The new property manager and the maintenance man got all over the newest tenant, in the family unit, over the big dog she has. It's not hers, it belongs to her boy friend. Then the maintenance man had it out with her boy friend. He did not want him hanging around here and says he looks like a bum. They are doing this and not taking care of multiple major things that are needed done here.

This was just another Friday afternoon when the maintenance man came and went down, to that same tenants unit, just to visit, for almost two hours, when he should be working, then left.

This am when I looked out my bedroom window the white skunk was walking along the sidewalk. Also the chickens and ducks were all over the lawn. The neighbors kid's toys were scattered all over the common area.

One tenant driving with an expired inspection sticker, on her van and an expired drivers license. When she renewed her license, the last time, it had been expired a year. Also she owes two months back rent. She keeps talking about going to the valley fund and getting them to give her money to pay the back rent. She's a procrastinator about everything. Now she got an eviction notice, from a lawyer. She has until the start of November, to pay up. Now she's finally going to make out the paperwork, for the valley fund, that she's had at least a month.

Now she's trying to get someone else to make out the paperwork. She says she does not know how to do it. She wants to just call them and tell what she wants. Not likely to happen.

Now we are having a glitch, in the telephone system. In the middle, of a call it goes dead, no dial tone. Waited and it came back. Other tenants having the same problem; but their phone has not come back. I called one tenant having the problem. It rang at least 20 times and the answering machine never came on. He said his phone never rang.

Finally the maintenance man came and set out traps, to catch all the cats that run loose around the complex. We have been complaining about the cats, for 6 years.

Maybe the new property manager is getting things done here. I gave her a full plus page of things we all have been complaining about, for 6 years. The sidewalk got fixed and traps set, to catch the tenants cats that they let run loose, all the time. But there's a lot more on the list that are even more important, to take care of.

Now I find out the traps are baited, to catch the skunks, not the cats. Am today two different cats running around here.

The maintenance man started clearing all those weeds with a walk behind brush hog. Only did part of it and left. He left the machine behind so I hope he's coming back and finishing. He came back for the machine; but never cleared anymore brush.

On weekends the women that has the chickens and ducks just lets them run loose, on the property. During the week they often get out, on their own.

At times the maintenance man has been seen picking up alcohol, for that tenant. She is often drunk for several days.

I just found out the drug dealer who used to come here, to sell drugs to tenants, was here a few days ago to see one tenant. Now she says she's missing money.

Newest news is the mother of one of the disability tenants was caught, on a surveillance camera stealing money, from the meals on wheels fund, at a convenience store.

Here's another day, Monday, and all the chickens and ducks are out all over the property. But no one from the owners are here to see it.

When you tell them they do nothing. Yet they told the women that owns them if they are out all over that they would get rid of them. Like always they never follow through with anything.

A neighbor, of that one that gets drunk. Said the other day she was so drunk that she fell down, in the back yard and could not get up.

This am two chickens and the white duck were outside my bedroom window. Picking at things, on the ground.

Newest happing this am. That drug dealer is back with my neighbor. They are outside the front door. He's wearing a neck brace and his left arm, is in a sling. Now she brought him back later and I heard her say he rolled his car and he's staying with her for a while. I noticed the owners about what went on. That nobody wants him here and does not belong here. Later when he came out his arm was not in a sling and he was using it. He just is a con man and she is so dumb that she believes him. Now a dirty low life friend of his has shown up. I hope he's not going to be hanging around, also. The two of them left together and his arm was back in the sling. He came back later and stayed with her. Last week when he came to see her she said he took some of her money and then she does this. I can not believe anyone would be this dumb.

As the day winds down now that drug dealer shows up with two cars full of low lifes. They sneak into the back of her unit area, and having a drinking party. They are turning this place right back to a rat hole. That's because the owners never inforce important things here. The sooner she's evicted the better off this place will be.

Why should the descent tenants have to put up with one tenant bringing these low lifes here. They are the low lifes of the area. They are nothing but drunks and drug addicts. One is a drug dealer. That's where the tenant gets her marijuana. If we had someone, from the owner's office here daily they would see the problems. But when it's reported, to them, they do nothing. That tenant has until November 1st., to pay the two months back rent she owes. We all hope she can not then they will follow through with her eviction. Her friend that was evicted from here and now in Florida. She was to go to Florida and live with him. Even he doesn't want her down their. We all want her out of here. Not so much for her as for the bums that constantly come here to see her. I'll be surprised if they do evict her. They never follow through with anything. The one they evicted and ended up in Florida. He owed a large amount of back rent and was doing criminal things to other tenants. They kept giving him eviction notices and gave him to much slack. It finally took them a year to get him out of here. Even after the state police arrested him and spent several days in jail.

That women that recently moved into the family unit, with her daughter. She had this new job only three weeks and just walked out and quit. Never gave them any notice. How is she going to pay her rent. She talks about going to Utah where her brother is. Where is she going to get the money to go there. We all believe she was fired.

That low life that's staying with the neighbor, has been evicted out of his place. So he will be staying with her. He probably is going to have surgery on his neck nerve as she says. With an injured shoulder, recovery will be a long time. Why should we have to put up with him being here.

Now the neighbor is talking about the two of them driving to Florida so she can be with that bum that was evicted from here. Also he's smoking, in her unit, in violation of the no smoking rule.

Now this am the chickens and ducks were out by the front door of my unit. The yellow cat was running around out there.

That low life, that's staying with my neighbor, is causing her all kinds of problems. But she won't throw him out. She is so dumb. Now she's taking him to get his pinched nerve checked, she has a therapy appointment she won't make and needs to go to the food shelf, for the food she needs. Now she says she has only two weeks to pay her back rent and doesn't have the money for next months rent also. She does not know how to fill out the paperwork to ask the valley fund for it.

I just heard that the MRI, that the low life had, showed he has no injuries. So it's all a con game to stay with her because he was evicted from his place.

One neighbor has his car parked half on the new sidewalk. The maintenance man was working ten feet away and never told him to move his car.

Well finally something has been done about that low life staying with my neighbor. The new project manager called her and read the riot act to her. He will be out of here in two days. She's in trouble about more things anyways. She went pounding on a neighbor's door accusing her of turning her in. Then came pounding at my door saying the same thing. I told her I hadn't talked to the project manager. It was the Tenants Association that notified the owners. The neighbor called the owners about this and they said just forget about it.

The Tenants Association sent a letter, from the decent tenants, complaining about that low life being here and that he was smoking, in her unit, against the complex rules. He first was going around without the sling, then not even wearing the neck brace. She still didn't get it. It was a con game so she would let him stay their. As was said he was evicted out of where he was living.

What she doesn't understand is that you can have someone else stay with you 24/7, up to 30 days. But you will have to notify the owners of that and pay an increase in the rent, for those 30 days. She didn't notify anyone or pay extra rent, for the two weeks he was there. The maintenance man new he was living their, with her. Also other tenants and the maintenance man heard her yelling about him smoking in the unit.

Neighbors said several evenings he was running around, like a crazy man. He most likely was high on drugs. As he's a known drug dealer, for years in the area.

If she doesn't pay her rent by the 5th. of October, then she will be three months behind in rent. Today is the day that low life was told to be out of here. I see him still here, out back of her unit, now again wearing that neck brace. It looks like he's going to try to pull a con, with the owners, so he can stay there.

I found out, that her neighbor's, the wife has cancer and they are complaining about smelling smoke from her unit. So there's been multiple complaints about him being here and of he is smoking in her unit against the complex rule of no smoking in apartments.

Multiple neighbors said he was running around outside half naked and running up the road. Lots of tenants driving, on the road passed him. So it was multiple complaints about him.

Now that tenant that drinks likes to expose herself to men tenants. Example; she calls her neighbor over and tells him she has something on her breast. Look at it and she pulls up her top and exposes herself to him. This has happened many times. One time she called me to fix something for her. Afterwards she said she had minor surgery. See where I had it and drops her jogging pants and of course she doesn't wear underwear.

Now that neighbor, that drinks, is at it again. She's back to telling lies about other tenants, to make trouble between tenants. But she is the one that's calling in complaints about others, to the owners office. And then saying someone else is the one that called in. It seems like she delights in making trouble.

Early am, when I opened my curtains, I noticed my neighbor across, her storm door was open, strange. Then I saw an EMT come out and close up. I went out and saw the tenant being loaded in the ambulance.

I see that women that lives in the family unit, with her daughter. She had quit a good job, at the condos, is now back working at the convenience store that she had quit there before.

The women that went this am, to the hospital, called me. They are keeping her. I had told her she needed an MRI to tell what's going on. She said the doctor asked her if she had had an MRI. The doctor made her an appointment at the spine clinic. She may have to have surgery. Depending on what the MRI shows. But her own doctor will have to make the appointment for the MRI.

One neighbor who has been fighting cancer for two plus years has had many surgeries. Lately he's gone to emergency every week and sometimes twice a week.

That women who received an eviction notice. Today she was arguing with her next door neighbor. She was so loud and waving her arms around. Now she's spreading stories that the fellow, that's been fighting cancer, has only three weeks to live. Other tenants have been calling him about that. He says no such thing is happing. In fact he was just talking to me about going deer hunting.

The neighbor that's waiting to have the MRI, they just sent her home with more pain pills. The one that accused her of turning her in and yelling at her and said all kinds of things to her. Shows up at the hospital and acts like she came to check on her. To see how she's doing, what a phony.

Now the weather is changing, fall is upon us. Getting cooler and the trees have changed to widespread fall colors. Having the start of mixed precipitation. Soon the white stuff will fall from the sky.

The maintenance man came and finally trimmed the trees, along the driveway. The broken, the dead and overhanging branches. But still haven't fixed the holes, in the road. The holes have gotten much larger and deeper. Some one is going to have an accident and the owners will be responsible.

Now that neighbor who got in trouble, with the owners, is now calling in complaints about others and blaming it on others. Just to get revenge for being caught herself.

Now she called the owners and asked when she goes to Florida, for a month, she wanted that low life drug dealer, to stay in her unit while she's gone. They said no, he has a criminal background.

Mid October, I awoke to a dusting of snow, already. Which continued off and on most of the day. Cold and windy out but going to get milder this week.

Sunday the septic service was here to pump put a tenant's toilet system, as it was clogged up. That night the ambulance took him to the hospital again. He has recurring health problems. Now they moved him to a larger hospital.

A neighbor has another broken window. He has had so many broken windows. He always blames it on his kids, when they visit. We all know it's him that breaks the windows. As he has a violent temper.

Well it's Friday and and the neighbor who got the eviction notice, her psychiatrist is at her unit, as usual on Fridays. But with her attitude he doesn't seem to be helping her. Probably because she's not telling him the truth.

My neighbor that's been fighting cancer, for 2 plus years, and multiple side effects. At one am he drove himself, to the hospital emergency room with internal problems. One of the problems he has is smelling cigarette smoke, from his neighbors on both sides. Which is in violation of the no smoking rule, in their unit.

We have all been complaining about the poor road conditions. It's full of holes and is a private road. So the land owners are responsible to maintain it. They had all summer, to at least fill the holes. Now the road is dangerous and someone is going to have an accident. It's late October and soon we will have snow and people coming in will not know there's big holes under the snow. So I wrote a letter, to the governor, explaining the problem and asked for his help, in making the owners fix the road.

Maintenance installed a 4x4 post, for new tenant's dish, for tv. He said he wants all dishes, off the roof and on posts. He has nothing to say about it. Dish came and updated my dish for better reception and another tenant. They just updated the one, on the roof, with a new updated one and I got a new DVR. It stayed, on the roof.

My neighbor has medical problems and asked me to drive him, to the hospital that's a long way off. As those are the doctors who have been dealing with him. He picked the worse day. Cold am and warmer later with heavy rain and high winds. It's a 1 ½ hour drive to the hospital. But everything went ok. He got his procedure done and just rain, no wind, coming home.

My letter, to the governor, about the road condition, at least I got a response, from the state. They called the owners about the poor condition of the road. Owners responded by saying they are working with the town, on it. You know how long that will take, maybe spring. We need a fix now before we get snow. The state called me and went over everything, with me. They have no jurisdiction so they wanted to know what I wanted the state to do. I said I'd hope the state would put some pressure, on the owners, to get it done now. She said she would call back and tell them she's from the governor's office and that the governor is aware, of the road problem. Also something needs to be done before we get snow and someone has an accident.

Once again the maintenance man came, in the company van and went by with a bag, from the local grocery store, and took it to that same tenant, then left. So he used the company van and his time, when he is supposed to be working, to pick up groceries, for that same tenant. She is often very drunk.

Had a letter, from the governor's office. He appreciated my feedback and if I need anything else don't hesitate to call. They forwarded my letter, to agency of Human Services. As they are equipped to handle my specific issues and they would be in contact, with me.

The septic system should be pumped out at least twice a year, spring and fall. When they had the concrete box open you could see it was packed full. That's because they never pumped it out, at all this year. Every two units outfall comes together and then to the main line and into the box. Mine is having a problem. Flushes slowly and I've plunged it and poured in buckets of hot water, to break up blockage. That usually works. Some improvement but not back to normal. I don't know what my neighbor puts down his toilet. Maintenance was here Sunday and everyone is having a problem. Maybe a break, in the line. He didn't even know where the cleanout was. I had to show him and loan him my shovel, to dig it up. Quickly there was water coming up. The septic service came and ran high pressure hose down the cleanout, it worked. It was blocked where all the lines come together from 6 units.

I found out all the chickens and ducks are gone somewhere, for the winter. We hope they never come back.

Noon today the ambulance came, for one of my neighbors. I was told that she was having migraines. She came back home, in four hours. We all believe she was just out of pain killers and wanted the hospital, to give her something. She wears a pain patch, takes pain pills and smokes marijuana.

Saturday and the maintenance man came only, in the company van, just to visit with that same tenant, not to do any work, then left.

My neighbor who has been fighting cancer, for a long time, is sick again. These things have been happening closer and closer together. He's not looking good.

Another neighbor that went through pneumonia and a collapsed lung. Has been having recurring problems and now in the hospital over a month.

It's Monday and the maintenance man is putting out things, for the winter. Then he does what he usually does. Takes that same tenant to do her personnel errands, in the owners company van. The maintenance man was here Tuesday and took that same tenant, in the company van, to do her personnel errands. Some day he will get caught, by the property manager and be fired. But he knows no one, from the owners are hardly ever here.

Finally the septic service came and pumped out the concrete box. Which has not been done, in a year. Also pumped out another box that has not been done in the 6 ½ years I've been here. It was about time.

Again when I went out to do errands and come home there's a nonresident parked in my space. There's very little resident parking spaces. I've been after the owners for years to put up resident only parking signs and signs where guest can park. Bit they have done nothing, as usual.

My neighbor that's dealing, with cancer, when I saw him on Saturday he did not look very good. He was going out with his girlfriend. Sunday I learned she had to push him around, in a wheelchair, where they went. Then Saturday night she had to take him, to the hospital; where he is now.

A neighbor that has two cats. The female is not fixed and had gotten out. Just learned the cat had six kittens, against the owner's policy of only fixed cats can be here, in the tenant's unit.

Other neighbors, the wife has cancer problems. She has been, in the hospital, for a week now.

Another thing that happens, on occasions. Is that when someone comes to visit a tenant, they bring their own laundry and use our washer and dryer. Because it's cheaper then going to the laundromat. There's only one washer and one dryer, for 12 units. So they are taking laundry time away from tenants. The owners policy is that the laundry facilities are for the tenants use only.

The neighbor that was in the hospital, came home. But he's keeping to himself. He still does not look very good. This am the visiting nurse came to see him. Also this day the ambulance took another tenant, to the hospital.

The agency of Human Services called me, in reference to the dangerous condition, of the road leading into the complex. There office has no jurisdiction as it being a private road. It would depend on the agreement made to make it a private road. It may tell who is responsible to maintain the the road and do any repairs. I will go to the town hall and check.

Again ten ants cats are out running around the complex.

In the past week three state police and one sheriffs cars have been here. They were up to the family unit area.

Early at 5 am I could see that the door, to the common room and laundry room had been open all night. This is not the first time and lights left on all night. Also it is December and 15 degrees out. That would make the heat work overtime trying to keep the room warm.

I had a long talk with the town manager about the dangerous conditions of the road leading into the complex. The owners called her and she told them since it is a private road the town is not responsible to repair it. The town manager let me look at all the files, on the complex. There was nothing about the road even in the original permit to build the complex. She also said there's no record agreement on the road. Which might have spelled out who is responsible for repairs. Usually it's the land owners along the road.

I wrote the governor's office and let them know where it all stands. I don't know if they called the owner's again. The property manager was here, to pick up rent checks. She said that they were in touch with a local contractor.

The outside lights have never worked correctly since new ones were installed a few years ago. Some come on and some don't. All lights come on then some go off. The maintenance man came just to change an outside bulb. A waist of man power and still the important things are not getting done.

Just another day where the maintenance man came and sat in the company van killing time. Then went down to visit that same tenant and left. Was not here to do any work.

It's more then a week since the property manager said they were in touch with a local contractor, to fix the road. So far the road has not been repaired. There is 24 units and why should we have to put up with driving through large holes and broken pavement every day. There own maintenance comes almost every day and has to drive through the road.

The secure door, to the boiler room, was left open over the weekend.

My neighbor who has been going through pains for months. They just kept giving her different pain pills without truly finding the cause. She had at times so much pain that the ambulance took her, to the hospital and they just gave her more pain pills. Well finally the doctor woke up and had her take an MRI to find what is wrong with her.

Another neighbor who has been dealing with health problems for months. Now has been in the hospital more then two months just passed away. This is the second neighbor that has passed away since I've been living here.

My next door neighbor keeps her apartment closed up ever since she moved in. Curtains are always closed and very rarely is a window open, even in the hot summer. She claims that she has no income and the state pays her rent.

This am I noticed spray paint markings, on the worst part of the road where our driveway starts. It's from dig safe as our power and telephone lines are underground. Hopefully that this means the road will finally get repaired. That waited long enough as it's mid December. So far no snow and mild temperatures.

The tenant across from me and is in a wheelchair, was trying to put up X-mas decorations and got up on a table and fell off and broke her foot. Since she has only one foot now she can not even drive her van.

It's Saturday and the maintenance man is here, in the company van. Not to do any work. Just to visit with that same tenant, for a long time.

I just found out the tenant that owed back rent and had received an eviction notice. She got $1,000.00, from the church, to pay her back rent. That's almost double what she owed. The rest she spent on herself. She owes her neighbor money. I hope she paid her back.

Here it is X-mas and it's 50 degrees out. I'm looking at green grass, no snow. Still the owners have not repaired the road. Next week it's suppose to be in the 30's with rain and mix precipitation.

When the owners evicted a low life tenant for not paying his rent. The night before the sheriff came, to lock him out of his apartment, he was running around drunk and stoned on drugs. He punctured the sidewalls, on three of my tires. I had to get three new tires. I'm lucky I have good vandalism insurance, on my car. The insurance company paid 100%, of the costs. When I first moved in here the same tenant punctured another tenants tires the same way twice. Since no one saw him do it, even though I showed it, to the state police, there was nothing they could do. One tenant said he saw him out by my car at 1:30 am but he would not testify to that. He also was on drugs with that same tenant.

Well it's the end of December and we finally got snow and freezing rain. Still the owners have done nothing to repair the dangerous road.

The tension here you could cut, with a knife. No one are talking to other tenants. Some tenants are just keeping closed up, in their apartment and avoiding others.

Am on the last day of December I see the door, to the common room has been wide open on a cold day.

The tenant who has been fighting cancer is in the hospital again with multiple problems, for a week.

It's January 6th and I see the underground utilities are again painted up. Maybe the road will finally be repaired.

The tenant that just spent a week, in the hospital, two days after he came home he's back, in the hospital.

It's the 7th of January and finally the contractor came and did the road repairs. This is the way the owners always operate. They don't take care of problems until something falls apart or you keep after them. They keep trying to put off what needs, to be done, as long as they can. They had all summer and a mild fall through December to repair the road. They are lucky that no one had an accident. Otherwise they would have a major lawsuit, on them.

It's Friday and as usual the tenant, across from me, her psychiatrist came to see her. Afterwards they were outside and she was arguing with him and waving her arms and pointing to other units. You could see he was lecturing to her.

After three days, in the hospital, that tenant is back in his unit again, but not looking good.

Just as I thought that I've seen everything that could happen here, I was wrong. It was a cold January evening and I was just going, to take a shower. When my neighbor called and said I'd better move my car as the car that's parked 10 feet, from mine, is on fire. I pulled on my joggers and stuck my feet in something and grabbed a coat. The flames were 4 feet high coming from the engine. The fire department was already here. I moved my car up to the family units and left it all night. Just incase the fire reignited. It's a wonder the gas tank didn't blow up. Earlier, in the day, two people were trying to get his car started.

It's starting again. I go out for a ½ an hour and some non-resident parks in my space. There's hardly enough parking spaces for the residents. It turned out it was the same person who parked, in my space, before and I had left her a note not to park here and she ignored it.

Now that burned out car has been sitting in front of the unit, for a week now. No signs of anyone trying to remove the car. Engine, dashboard and front seat burned out. Front tires melted.

Some time ago there was a rehab done at this complex. They hired a 3rd rate contractor who has done the worse job I've ever seen. They dug up the foundation to insulate with blue board. The small backhoe broke and dented siding all over and never repaired the siding. They did an incomplete job and skipped areas and took every shortcut they could. The owner's manager went along with what they did. She had some book learning but not even one minute of construction experience. She also was arrogant to some tenants. I still believe the contractor was paying her off, to look the other way. When it rains against the siding the water ran down and to the ground. Now, with the blue board, the rain runs under the siding, which was never caulked and into some unit floors. When they trimmed the siding they left it jagged and open spaces. One day I saw a big grass snake come out of my units siding, from the space left open. As for the windows when they took them out they never removed old caulking and shims. Just jammed the new ones in and never caulked the outside space before they put in the finished edges.

As for the front door. They replaced it with the same rated door that was in there. I've replaced many door units. It always only took me 2 to 2 ½ hours to remove the old unit and put in a new one. It took them over 6 hours and was done wrong. They never put anything under the threshold plate, so it bends and never sealed it from the cold. Then spent several hours more just to put back the door trim and finish work.

This afternoon some guy knocked at my door. He handed me a basket with chips etc. in it. Then he wanted to come in and bring others to talk I said no and handed back his basket. Very suspicious. Owners should post this place against such people coming around. He never even said what he wanted, to talk about. He said he was the manager but never said manager of what.

It's now weeks since that car burned up. It is still sitting in front of his unit. There's been no attempt to move it. The owners have made no attempt to make him move the car or do it themselves. It may still be there in the spring. That's the usual way the owners work.

I see they cleared a path, through the snow, at the back doors of the 12 senior units. That's a fire safety law. Usually I have to call and tell them if they don't clear the path I will call the state fire marshal and the owners will be fined and still have to clear the path, so do it.

Early am on Sunday my neighbor and his girlfriend came home. He had a white cover wrapped around him. Like they give you at the hospital. So he went Saturday night, to the hospital. This is the 4th time in two weeks.

That tenant's car that burned up weeks ago, is still sitting in front of his unit. But since the fire there's been no sign, of the tenant.

The tenant that past away, in the hospital, about 6 weeks ago. His family has come around to move his things, from the apartment.

The tenant that's been fighting cancer, for so long is not doing good. His girlfriend has quit her job so she can be with him a lot of the time. I found out, from his girlfriend, he's in lot worse condition then we all thought.

It's the last weekend, in January, and I see there's a U-Haul up at one of the family units. So someone is moving out.

I was going to do my laundry but I found the washing machine is not working.

In the summer a lot of people, that don't live here, come in and throw their trash, in our dumpster. That's why it was always overflowing. Even some people who come to visit a tenant throw their trash, in our dumpster.

When the owner's have there yearly inspection, of the units, tenants have been written up for violations. But they never follow through and make the tenant take care of the problems. One tenant has so much junk, in the living room. You can hardly walk around. It's a major fire trap. Also junk blocking part of both entrances. Also junk piled against the building front and back. Maintenance came and cleared anything touching the building and totally ignored that tenant's junk.

Today it's warm and heavy rain and someone is spreading a lot of salt, on the sidewalk, which will never work, another waste.

At 4:30 am this morning the ambulance, with flashing lights, was here. A second ambulance came. But the tenant that's been fighting cancer for so long was taken to the hospital in extreme pain.

Finally, after almost a month, that burned out car has been removed. But no one cleaned up the burned out parts, on the ground. Some of them are metal and with snow covering them someone will drive over the parts and maybe get a flat tire.

Cats running loose again. One I'd never seen before.

I just found out the tenants that moved out, of the family unit, the end of January was evicted for owing back rent.

It's almost mid February and in the local newspaper an article about the other complex that they own, in the same town, tenants reported bed bugs. They could not get in touch with the property manager. When they finally got in touch with the overall property manager, she was very slow to respond to the tenants problems. Only when the tenants got in touch with the town health officer, who told the owners that they are in violation of state law, did the owners respond to the problem and finally had a service come and work on the bed bug problem.

Mid February we have 5" of snow covered with an inch of ice and raining. The snow removal service came and plowed the road in and up by the family units. Never plowed where my car and three other neighbors park, so we could get out, if we need to. They never shoveled the walkway. I talked to the maintenance man and he's going to make a call, to the service. He also said that the owners had the burned out car removed and will bill the tenant. This am the ambulance came and took that same tenant, to the hospital. Also the maintenance man said the burned out car was not in the name of the tenant. Also he had no car insurance and that the battery was connected wrong.

The secure door, to the boiler room, has again been left open all night.

The road coming in and the driveway, in the complex, are share ice. You can't even walk on it. They finally came and sanded, but there was so little sand you couldn't see it. The next day everything was right back to share ice and no sign of sand. It's 45 degrees today and above freezing tonight and tomorrow in the 40's. But the service is loading up the sidewalk with salt that won't work, at those temperatures. Just another waste. These kind of wastes go on all the time.

Some day all this will catch up with the people, in the office, and they all will be looking for a job.

Well this is another day when the maintenance man came and spent several morning hours at that same tenants apartment. He was not doing repairs. He was working on doing personal fixing for her, not related to his job. Anytime she wants anything she calls him on his cell phone and runs right here. Others who put in a legitimate work order have to wait before he comes.

My neighbor that has been dealing with cancer for such a long time, is back in the hospital again. There are so many health issues with him that his future doesn't look good. He's on 2 hour pain medication and has lost so much weight, over the course of everything. He is at a critical stage.

Now we have a power outage and it's pouring rain outside.

That tenant came home after 1 ½ weeks, in the hospital. The doctors said there's nothing they can do for him. So it's just a matter of time before something happens to him.

Now that the weather is staying nice tenants cats are running loose around the complex again.

It's Saturday and the maintenance man is here, with the company van. Just to bring, to that same tenant, milk and other groceries, not part of his job.

Today was HUD's yearly random inspection of units. It was a bigger joke then the owner's yearly unit inspections.

The tenant that has the cancer. One day he's in such bad shape it looked like he might not make it. Then the next day he's like that had never happened.

Here it is the end of March and now we are getting snow after the mildest winter ever and almost no snow this winter. But in two days it's going to be in the 60's.

The ambulance is here today. We have a tenant who smokes marijuana and gets drunk, at the same time. Then she throws up to a point of being dehydrated. Then she calls 911 and goes to the hospital. She's always back, in a couple of hours. She has done this multiple times a year. She is often drunk on a regular basis.

My neighbor that's been going through the cancer and other health problems. Said he and his girlfriend are looking for a place, for the both of them, closer to the hospital. When he's in pain the ride from here, to the hospital, makes his condition worse.

Now we have another power outage. Also the phone is out.

There's an older couple and the wife has been going through several cancer problems. Now she has lung cancer and hospice has been coming now. If she passes on I don't know if the husband will stay. It's a two bedroom unit. There is still a one bedroom unit empty, in my section.

There has been an empty unit, in my section, since November. When the tenant passed away, in the hospital. I hear finally there is a man going to move into the unit. He is a local and I know who he is. He has a reputation of being a drunk. Just what we don't need. Just when things quiet down the owners do this. They just don't do enough of a background check on new tenants.

Also a new family moved into the empty family unit. They are driving a new expensive SUV and they were seen unloading fancy furniture. How could they qualify to be a low income family? This complex is supposed to be for people who can't afford regular rentals.

Here it is the 5th of April. Now we get a dusting of snow and colder temperatures then we had this past winter.

It's Friday afternoon and the maintenance man is here to take that same tenant, in the company van, to do her personal errands. He was not here to do any work.

Today the ambulance came and took the tenant, in the end unit, to the hospital. His old girlfriend is there 24/7 and pregnant from some other guy. She is not allowed to stay there. Also the next door tenant says they yell and argue until 1 am and keep her awake. Also again there is a car, at his unit, with no license plates. So it's unregistered. The last time it took the owners more then six months to get them to remove the last car. It didn't run, unregistered, and no inspection sticker and sat there at least 8 months.

The tenant that's been fighting cancer spent another night in the hospital. Second time in a week.

Last night a bear got into the dumpster and torn up garbage bags are all over.

In the middle of the day a large groundhog ran down the sidewalk.

I have a neighbor whose life is like a soap opera. She had planned to drive, to Florida, soon. Alone in her van to visit the low-life they evicted out of the complex and now living in Florida. At first she thought she had refractured her hip and she said now she will never get to Florida. It turned out it was a pulled ligament and the doctor gave her muscle relaxers. The fellows son was to send him money so he could send it to her to pay her expenses, for the trip. Well that didn't happen so now she has to take out a second loan, on the van. But the van is in her son's name as she has no credit. To get a loan he will have to transfer ownership to her. With her poor credit, the present loan they will raise the loan rate if it's in her name. Which makes her payments larger. Also the fellows son was to buy him a condo or a house. Which won't happen. So now he has to look for a two bedroom apartment with a years lease. That will put off her trip. She can't get it through her head he is just scamming her. No one believes he even wants her in Florida, with all her problems.

It looks like the bear got into the dumpster again. Torn up garbage bags all over, again.

The tenant in the end unit; there is him, his girlfriend and four kids and ones a two month old baby. They also say she's pregnant, by some guy. Two kids are his and the other two are hers by different men. The kids run loose with no supervision. Two of them and a trouble maker kid, from one of the family units, had sticks and banging on a car. None of them should be here. This area is not the family section. There toys and lots of their other things are all over the common area. Owners are never here to see what goes on. When they are they do nothing. I now hear that they all are moving soon, to the trailer park, I hope so.

There is two sections of siding that fell off, again, in the wind. Two months ago and laying, on the ground. The maintenance man has been here multiple times and didn't put the siding back up.

Last night the bear was back. Torn up garbage bags and the sliding door was ripped off the dumpster.

The neighbor that's been fighting cancer is back in the hospital again. He was, in the hospital several days. The day after he got back home he went fishing.

Here it is April 26th and we got snow. Four inches of heavy wet snow.

The day the kids were running loose and banging on things, with branches. One of them broke off the light on a post along the sidewalk.

The older couple living here. The wife has lung cancer and now she's in a hospital bed, at home and on oxygen. Two days later she passed away. These things happen when you live in senior housing.

Now the same tenant is back telling lies about other tenants. Making up stories and making trouble between other tenants. Everyone is tired of her antics. This has created tension for tenants unnecessary. She has no life, no interest and spends her time watching others and telling stories about them. She's been telling false stories, to the project manager, about what other tenants are doing and reporting tenants when there's no cause to do so. Also most of what she reported was none of her business and had no proof of what she was telling. She claims she stopped smoking. But she was seen buying a carton of cigarettes. Her neighbor says late at night they still smell smoke coming from her apartment. So she's in violation, of the rules. She's been seen smoking out back of her unit.

My neighbor is back, in the hospital again. With the same problem.

Well last night the bear was here again. He got into the dumpster and there was torn up garbage bags, by the dumpster.

The owners are building another public housing complex, in the southern part of the state. They are not taking care of this place properly. With another complex they will do even less here then before. They are more interested in expanding their base, then taking care of what they got. In the past the maintenance man is here sometime almost every day. Now we haven't seen him, except once, in the past two weeks. Grass is getting long and thick and no sign of the service mowing yet.

The tenant with all those kids and his girlfriend living here. Nothing but kids yelling and causing problems. There things are all over the place and on the sidewalk. He lets them run loose with no supervision. He's always yelling and disturbing his neighbor to the point that she doesn't get any sleep. But she won't complain because she's afraid he might do something. As he tends to be violent some times and is always yelling and swearing. His kids went into the common room and pulled a pile of big leaves off a nice big plant and through them on the floor. They also turned on the hot water, in the common room bathroom and left it running all day. That made 6 units with no hot water. The maintenance man had to come at night to find out what the problem was.

This am early there was a white skunk outside my bedroom window.

Here it is May 16th and we are getting a dusting of snow. Warm up coming this week, in the 70's.

They finally came and mowed the lawn. The grass in some places was a foot tall. The rest was more then 6 inches tall. You could cut it for hay.

Three days later they came and mowed the grass again. They raked up piles of cut grass, in the area of the leaching field. But didn't rake up where tenants have flower gardens and walk over the grass, all the time.

It's now more then three months that car has been sitting, by a unit. With no license plates or inspection sticker. It looks like someone took off the inspection sticker and may have put it on another car. As it was still good for 6 months more.

Now they took the plates off an old car and put it on the one sitting there. They did go to the DMV and transfer the registration, as they said. In that unit there's 4 kids. Two of them are always climbing out the window and running around.

Now a tenant has been cited, for the third time, for smoking in her unit. There rule says three citations means an eviction notice for violating the rules of no smoking in units. But there general rules say three citations within three months is subject to eviction. Two of her notices were more then three months ago. So we will see what rules the owners use. I bet they do nothing, as usual.

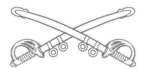

Well last night the bear was here again. He got into the dumpster and there was torn up garbage bags, by the dumpster.

The owners are more interested in expanding their base, then taking care of what they got. In the past the maintenance man is here sometime almost every day. Now we haven't seen him, except once, in the past two weeks. Grass is getting long and thick and no sign of the service mowing yet.

The tenant with all those kids and his girlfriend living here. Nothing but kids yelling and causing problems. There things are all over the place and on the sidewalk. He lets them run loose with no supervision. He's always yelling and disturbing his neighbor to the point that she doesn't get any sleep. But she won't complain because she's afraid he might do something. As he tends to be violent some times and is always yelling and swearing. His kids went into the common room and pulled a pile of big leaves off a nice big plant and through them on the floor. They also turned on the hot water, in the common room bathroom and left it running all day. That made 6 units with no hot water. The maintenance man had to come at night to find out what the problem was.

This am early there was a white skunk outside my bedroom window.

Here it is May 16th and we are getting a dusting of snow. Warm up coming this week, in the 70's.

They finally came and mowed the lawn. The grass in some places was a foot tall. The rest was more then 6 inches tall. You could cut it for hay.

Three days later they came and mowed the grass again. They raked up piles of cut grass, in the area of the leaching field. But didn't rake up where tenants have flower gardens and walk over the grass, all the time.

It's now more then three months that car has been sitting, by a unit. With no license plates or inspection sticker. It looks like someone took off the inspection sticker and may have put it on another car. As it was still good for 6 months more.

Now they took the plates off an old car and put it on the one sitting there. They did go to the DMV and transfer the registration, as they said. In that unit there's 4 kids. Two of them are always climbing out the window and running around. His girlfriend may be pregnant.

My neighbor that's been fighting cancer problems. He had an appointment to have a stint changed. He and his girlfriend went two days ahead and got a motel and planned on a nice dinner and doing something before their appointment. That first night he was in so much pain and a temperature of 100+ and incoherent. They went right to the hospital. He had a bladder and kidney infection. They will have to clear that up before they can change the stint. So he will be at the hospital awhile.

Another tenant took her electrical wheelchair to be repaired. When she tried to come home the transmission on her van went. She had to have it towed back a long distance.

A new tenant moved into the empty one bedroom unit. He is a local and has a reputation of being a drunk and a pain in the neck. We all know him and don't want to have anything to do with him. His son came, in a pickup truck, with some of his furniture. He parked in a handicap parking space. A tenant tried to tell him he can't park there and the tenant will be back soon. He mouthed off to the tenant. So already his presents here is causing trouble.

There's a tenant in a family unit that is supplying other tenants with marijuana. I can see that drug use here has begun to escalate again. I know of at least three tenants, in my section, that use marijuana. They all smoke it inside against the owners rule of no smoking in units.

Now I see someone bringing furniture, for the new tenant, drove over the leaching field and parked at his front door.

Everyone is back to causing trouble for others. They tell things about other tenants and then that gets repeated. Then the original person gets mad because a tenant told another tenant and they didn't want anyone else to know.

Now the new tenant parked on the new sidewalk, in front of his door, to unload his stuff. Then later he parked in another tenants parking space. Causing a long time tenant to find another parking space. The owners have been notified of the problem he's causing. We will see if they do anything. There usual is to sit on their hands until they have no choice.

That tenant that was in the hospital for five days with serious conditions. The day after he came home he went fishing. It was like nothing ever happened.

The siding that's been on the ground for at least three months. The tenants son put it back up because there was no sign that the maintenance man was going to do it.

The maintenance man was here and all he did was take the garbage, for that same tenant, to the dumpster.

The tenant that was in the hospital is having more problems. He is reacting to all the antibiotics he got in the hospital.

A neighbor who is in a wheelchair has a woman come from the county agency to clean her unit. Now the woman is bringing her boyfriend right into the unit while she cleans. He looks like someone that may be homeless. If the agency new she would be fired.

Because of the owners slow reaction to take care of problems caused by the new tenant. He has made more problems. When a tenants son was visiting the new tenant hit his car. Police were called and of course he denied it. But his right front had new fresh marks and matching paint, to the car hit. His car has multiple small damage from other minor accidents. Typical of a drunk which is his reputation. Also he was seen by other tenants peeking into his neighbors windows.

This was all discussed with three tenants and the property manager. One of the tenants is the one that saw him peeking in the windows. Basically the manager is just going to call him about this. We wanted an official letter from the owners to him. A call is their usual joke. It won't mean anything. Basically the owners are going to do nothing, as what they do all the time.

The tenant with all those kids had some kind of a water play thing for them. But he left the hose all along the sidewalk where someone could trip over it. He always leaves everything all over and never picks up anything. He's handicapped and drives with hand controls. He drove out of here like a maniac and with all these kids playing in the complex. Also he broke his apartment fire extinguisher and stole the one out of the common room.

Early am the EMT was here, for a tenant. She smokes marijuana and gets drunk. Then keeps throwing up until she gets dehydrated and calls 911. Then she walks to the ambulance and always back in a few hours. She's done this over and over again.

The tenant with all those kids is also in a wheelchair. His parking space is at his front door. When he came home people visiting the new tenant was parked in his space. He went and asked them to move and they refused to move.

The property manager new of all the problems with the new tenant before he signed the lease and still let him in. She was told he was fired from driving a taxi and from the transit company that takes people to medical appointments. Also he passed out drunk at the doctors office. Also multiple problems he caused for other people.

Now the road they repaired is full of holes again. They need to take care of the road. The project manager and the maintenance man come here multiple times and drive through these holes and do nothing to fix the problem.

A visitor parked in a tenants parking space. The tenant called the property manager and complained. She told him that there's no assigned parking spaces. That anyone can park anywhere including visitors. She told him to find another place to park. He's in a wheelchair. Just another demonstration that the property manager is worthless. Why should a tenant have to find another parking space because a visitor parked in his space. Don't tenants have any rights anymore? You can see one new worthless tenant can ruin everything for long time residents.

The Tenants Assoc. has written HUD about all this. Also just sent a follow up letter to HUD with a lot more problems that the new tenant is causing and it shows the property manager is worthless.

The tenant with all those kids had a birthday party. He left all the things all over the common area. Including the kids diaper.

Somebody climbed through the window, in the common room and made a mess. Left trash and cans all over.

The tenant with all those kids was drinking hard cider and rolled his wheelchair, in the parking area, on purpose. Then yelling he's going to sue the owners. The ambulance took him to the hospital where was found he had a fracture.

The tenant that's been fighting cancer for so long. Had a reaction to all the different medications he's taking. He went to the hospital but was back in a couple of hours.

The tenant with all those kids is telling everyone he had already given a 60 days notice of moving. He says he was approved to buy a trailer and put it in the local park. The maintenance man says he knows of no notice to move or an order to get a pad ready, in the park. We all were happy he was moving. But it looks like it's not true. As he's told fake stories before.

The new tenant woke up other tenants at early am hammering.

They finally had the road graded and the holes filled. They said they will be back to do more.

The tenant with all those kids should have never been allowed in here. To show what kind of a family he has. His mother has been picked up for DUI more then once. She was staying with her parents and was drunk and punched her father and he went, to the hospital, with a heart attack. She also exchanged punches with her mother and then took off. No one has seen her.

A tenant in a family unit has let her boyfriend's mother move in with her 24/7. But trying to keep it quiet as if the owners new she would have to pay extra rent, for the woman staying there.

The tenant that's fighting cancer left Sunday before 7am in a wheelchair. His girlfriend went flying out of here with him, in her car. Headed for the hospital emergency. He came back later that same day. He had another infection and another prescription.

The new tenant was seen driving all over the leaching field. It's a very shallow system and the weight of a car could break the pipes.

The new tenant was heard Sunday morning yelling and arguing with another tenant. From information gathered a tenant was leaving and the new tenant just pulled out without looking and cut off the other tenant. When I came home and was unloading my car he came home and staggered back to his unit. He was drunk.

The tenant with all those kids. His girlfriend left after he accused her of cheating on him. But other tenants reported that there was many woman coming and going from his unit, it was obvious that they were prostitutes.

The bear was here twice over the weekend. He ripped the door off the dumpster to get into the garbage.

Maintenance man was here, in the afternoon, just to visit with that same tenant and not to do any work. The property manager was here and went to the unit where all those kids live. They didn't open the door but one kid did and they closed the door on her. Then she just drove away. What a useless manager. I've been told they are behind in rent again.

The latest news is that a tenant is going to be evicted. Also the newer tenants in a family unit don't like living here. I saw them giving the manager an earful about something.

The tenant with the cancer problems is in the hospital again. This is the 3rd time in less then two weeks. Not a good sign. He didn't look good when he came home.

The tenant with all those kids. One of the kids was pulling up a tenant's granddaughters dress and looking under her. The tenant came out yelling and threatened to blow up my car because I stopped it. Later he apologized to me for the threats. But all of this was reported, to the manager. There was two other tenants who heard all this. One was the grandmother of the little girl. The manager had asked to be notified of any incident. But that doesn't mean she will do anything, as usual.

Two of the family units the tenants are dealing drugs. You can see a stream of cars in and out of the complex. They go to the unit for 5 minutes, for a buy.

The woman in a family unit, with a 3 year old girl, has been letting her boyfriends mother stay there. When she was staying with her boyfriend his mother let 5 people come in, for the night. The next door tenants said around midnight two people were having sex on the picnic table outside, the unit.

I left a message on the manager's answering machine. Telling her the word around the complex is that we have drug dealers here again. Living in both units 17 and 18. Also she needs to check this out. I will see if she follows through and contacts the state police.

When I came home there was a car in my parking space. It was someone visiting the new tenant. I went down and pounded on his door and told him to move his car. He didn't give me any lip, like he's done to others. Maybe because I was wearing my pistol and my handcuffs. It made an impression on him. Now maybe he will think twice about parking in my space.

The tenant with cancer spent another night at emergency, at the hospital.

The bear was in the dumpster again.

The tenant with all those kids. His girlfriend walked out, on him, again. She took her two kids with her. Maybe this time she won't be back. He goes off the wall and belligerent to her, his mother and the kids. He swears and yells at all of them. He still owes four months back rent, again. I hope this time the owners evict him. His girlfriend was giving him her whole disability check. Now he won't have that money.

The bear was in the dumpster last night, again. A mess of garbage all over. When are the owners going to contact fish and wildlife to try to trap the bear. This time the bear got into both dumpsters.

Still no sign of the property manager doing anything about all the complaints of what's going on or taking care of any problems. Tenants have called and she was at her desk and never answered their calls or called anyone back. That shows how useless she is.

The unmarked sheriffs car was here this afternoon. Checking out the area where units 17 and 18 are. The word has been that they are drug dealers.

The tenant with all those kids, the vehicle in front of his unit he says isn't working. Someone took off the valid inspection sticker. Probably put it on another car, illegal. The license plates has never had a valid date sticker, to show it's registered.

We got some good news, from the owners. The worthless property manager is leaving, with very little notice. Probably because she got fired.

Sunday am, I can see the bear has been in both dumpsters. Garbage all over, at both dumpsters.

The tenant with all those kids. His girlfriend came back with her two kids. He gave her an engagement ring. He finally got rid of that car that wasn't running. He sold it and instead of paying the four months or more back rent he owes. He bought the ging and a bunch of things, for the kids. Now he's back yelling, at his girlfriend and calling her a whore, again. Just after he gave her the ring. Earlier today I saw the drug dealer, from a family unit, come to see him.

His neighbor said he's back yelling half the night, at all the kids. So she can't get any sleep.

My neighbor fell, in the grass and couldn't get up. Another tenant came out and yelled for me. She is very, very hefty and it took a lot to get her back on her feet. At least she had no injuries.

The woman in a family unit, with a 3 year old daughter. Her mother just turned 61, my neighbor. She gave her marijuana for a birthday present. That's because she and her low-life boyfriend smoke it. What a family.

Since I've been here we have had four property managers. On the am news they showed the owners opening a new complex. That's all they are interested in and not taking care of what they have.

The maintenance man was here today, to clean up the garbage, that the bear dragged out of the dumpster. There was trails of garbage through a path the bear made and into the woods. There was a large pile of spor and it was very black. So the bear is getting into the blackberries. The fish and wildlife was called but they won't come and trap the bear. So they ordered a bear proof dumpster.

This complex has gone back to being a rat hole. All the complaints by multiple tenants, to the owners, falls on deaf ears.

Sunday am when I walked up the path, to town, I saw the bear that's been getting into our dumpster. It's a young bear. But maybe there is an older bear also. The bear was about 50 feet from me. I had my pistol ready in case he got aggressive. But he turned and left the area.

Monday am I see the bear was in the dumpster again. Maintenance came and cleaned up all the garbage that was spread all over the field, by the bear.

Now again my neighbor is talking about going to Florida to see that low-life that was evicted out of here. With all the goings on she can't see that's he lying to her about everything and doesn't want her in Florida. She's been talking she needs to go now because of the health problems he says he has. Which is a lie. Said he had two strokes and a heart attack but never went to the hospital. He was to send her money, on the third but here it is the 17th and no money. Now she says she may not get there for six months. So she can't be so worried about him, as she says.

Tuesday when I went out, after 8am, there was no sign the bear had been here. But when I came back about 10:30 am there was garbage all over. So now the bear is coming in daylight hours. I saw a woman pushing a baby carriage and a young kid with her, coming down the path. What if they met the bear?

The tenants girlfriend that left with all four kids. The word is she's never coming back. After he gave her an engagement ring he called her all kinds of nasty things. She's the mother of all four kids but he's the father of only the two older ones. Seems like after he sold the car that didn't run, now he has a van. He got it somewhere. The body is in poor condition. Places have tape on the body. The word is the girlfriend called, where his mother works, and told the owners she was stealing. That got her fired.

Early Sunday morning there was a small white skunk outside my bedroom window.

The latest is the ones in unit 17, that have 7 cats, an 11 year old girl that visits, got infected with fleas. The maintenance man said both units 17 and 18 are being evicted, followed by an apartment inspection. He will get rid of all the fleas.

The tenant that has been fighting cancer, he went to the hospital, in the night with problems. He came home early am and then had to go back the next night, with the same problems.

The contractor came and fixed the road and driveway from the rain washouts. Also filled all the holes in the paved private road coming into the complex. About time the owners had the holes fixed. We have been waiting all summer for the repairs, to the holes.

So far I've not seen any activity of getting rid of those drug dealers, in the family units. Typical of the owners of slow reaction to everything they do.

This am now no phone service. Can't get any dial tone, on the phone. Also internet is out and the problems are wide spread, in the area. Stopped at the phone company and told them. At one point a phone truck came twice and just looked around and did nothing. By the next mourning the phone was back.

Friday am I see the bear has been into the new bear proof dumpster. Garbage all over the area and in the field. It looks like someone who put their garbage, in the side sliding door, did not latch the chain. Because nothing was broken.

Sunday I see there is a U-Haul truck up at the family units where those drug dealers are. So it does look like they have been evicted and moving out.

One tenant twice the same tire was low, on air. It got pumped up and fine and then over night it's down again. It looks like someone maybe letting the air out.

A neighbor was having pains and thought she had stones again. Early am she called me, from the hospital, it was her appendix, and it was leaking. So a quick surgery was done, to remove it. She came home the next day.

One tenant has been letting her cat out 24/7 when it wants out. Which is in violation of the complex rules. It sprays other tenants flower gardens and vegetable gardens. It's been catching and killing birds and chipmunks. The owners have been notified if they don't stop her from letting her cat out, that it will vanish and never be seen again.

Now someone stole a tenants handicap sign right out of the ground.

The tenant that had the appendix surgery now has a problem in her right shoulder. Express care said it was tendernightess.

The tenant with those kids. Now he's threatening everyone over nothing. He borrowed something and was told to bring it right back. Then he started yelling and threatening other tenants. Over the last year he's done this multiple times. He also owes two months back rent and has no money to pay this months rent. Why haven't they evicted him by now? Now I find out he can't find his drivers license. Now he's running his mouth about other tenants and saying he has lots on them. He's in a wheelchair, from a car accident, so he knows the owners will have trouble evicting him and he thinks he can get away with everything with no repercussions, because of that. The tenant that told him to bring it right back can't mind her own business. It had nothing to do with her but she always sticks her nose in everything and it often makes problems for other tenants. Also it put me in the middle when I had nothing to do with it. Just because she and I are friends. He apologized to her and and then she goes right over, to his unit, with her granddaughter, for a bbq. Like nothing ever happened. She's done this kind of thing before. She has no sense especially with all the things she's said about him and wants him out of here also.

The aggravation level here is high. There's always someone creating problems that affect other tenants. The owners turn a deaf ear to all the complaints, from tenants.

Now someone doing a to large a load, in the washer, brock the door seal so water leaks on the floor. It's Friday late afternoon, so who knows when it will get fixed.

This is the first Sunday, in a long time, that it's been quiet, in the complex. Maybe since some tenants are out of here and the one with the biggest foul mouth has been gone all day.

That tenant is still letting her cat out. We don't know if the owners called her about it or if she is ignoring the owners.

One tenant that finally left his family unit. The maintenance man was cleaning it out. He left with a trailer full of some furniture but with multiple upon multiple trash bags full of garbage and more. He said the unit was full of fleas.

Early am the big black and white skunk was walking along the sidewalk.

Wednesday they finally came and fixed the washer

Something new has come to light. The tenant with those kids is now dealing in drugs. Mostly now he hides out in his unit. We just got rid of the drug dealer, in a family unit, now this. The owners have no idea what goes on here. He has alienated everyone here at one time or another. By running his foul mouth to other tenants.

We had a surprise. The tenant who has been fighting cancer for a long time just married his caregiver.

The tenant that's been waiting for the results of her MRI, on her spine, now had right arm problems. She has found out that it's her rotor cup. That might require surgery plus she may have surgery, on her spine, for a possible pinched nerve. She seems that she has so many medical problems to deal with. After physical therapy it looks like no surgery on the rotorcup. Doctor said the MRI showed the fluid between vertebra has mostly gone causing her pains. No surgery but a different physical therapy, on her back and a pain patch for her pain.

We heard the owners hired a new property manager. The man was working for the county services. I hope this one is better than the last one. She was totally useless and did nothing in the year she had the job.

The latest event is the tenant with those kids had only one friend until he made lewd remarks about his wife. Now he has absolutely no friends. He should be evicted for multiple reasons. He also ran over the power cord, for his electric wheelchair. So he can't charge it and no longer can use it.

Over the weekend there was a stabbing at the unit of the other drug dealer, in a family unit.

This is the second time, in a short time, that the washing machine is not working. The clothes were not even wet, no water. A call was made, to the service, about it. The owners of the complex nearby just got new machines, why not us? Their new machines cost half the price to do there laundry then ours does.

The tenant that's been fighting cancer is back in the hospital with the same problem again that's been sending him, to the hospital, multiple times. He was to come home but had a relapse. He had so intense pain that they kept him longer. His wife now has an illegal handicap sticker, on her car, so she can park in a handicap space, at the complex.

The new property manager was shown around the complex but never talked to anyone. We were told he left his other job because there was to many things to deal with all the time. He's in for a rude awakening. Wait until he has to deal with all the crap here and some of these worthless tenants.

The tenant that's been fighting cancer. He went to the hospital, with the same problem. Only hours after he came home he was in such extreme pain the ambulance took him back, to the hospital. Where he stayed for several days.

The tenant with those kids has said awful, foul mouth things to another tenant. Then he calls her and asks her to bring him cigarettes and she does. It seems like she rather be with low-lifes then with decent people. It was found out she did that because she can get marijuana from him. This brings a new light to what is going on, in the complex. So we, for sure, have another drug dealer living here.

That recent new tenant that's a drunk. Today when I was parking my car he backed out and almost hit me. He didn't even know I was there. That's how much he's in a stopper all the time.

Now the tenant with those kids is openly trying to sell marijuana to other tenants. The new property manager has been notified, from the Tenant's Association, of this new problem. We all hope now the owners will finally evict him and if they contact the police he may get arrested, we hope..he has two young sons who live there and he's trying to get full custody. Bad influence for the kids and should not have any custody of them. He also smokes cigarettes and marijuana inside his unit which is in violation of the owners rules.

The new property manager called and when he's on property, in two days, that he will confront that tenant about trying to sell drugs, to other tenants. I hope that this results in that tenant getting evicted. Property manager said without proof of him selling the marijuana the police won't get involved without real evidence. Well both property managers were here today with maintenance to do clean up. But he never confronted the drug dealer. So nothing has changed and business as usual. So this hot shot big deal new manager is no better then the other ones we had. The owners are totally worthless. That tenant came over to bum cigarettes from my neighbor and she said he was stoned on drugs. His two boys had just come home from school.

Another tenant and their family are moving out of their family unit. That leaves several empty family units.

That tenant tried to sell marijuana, to another tenant, for $150.00. That tenant turned him into the owners and still they didn't do anything about him. He also told the tenant he keeps it in his refrigerator.

Again the maintenance man is back to his old ways. He took that same tenant to do her personal errands in the company van. Later went and brought her back groceries. Not here to do any work.

Someone is dumping old furniture by our dumpster. Maybe someone from the outside is coming in here at night and dumping. The owners are going to put up a camera, to catch the ones. The owners have to take it to recycling and pay for it. Also there was bags of garbage thrown behind the dumpster. The maintenance man found an empty pill bottle, in the garbage, with the name of that tenant with those kids.

The maintenance man said they are going to raise and improve the area I park and mark the parking spaces per unit. I've been asking for this for more then 7 years. Because sometimes when I come home a visitor is parked in my space. Then I have to find out where they are and get them to move their car.

Somebody again is throwing their garbage outside the dumpster. The maintenance man told that tenant, with the kids, to stop throwing his garbage bags outside the dumpster. It's possible that the furniture, at the dumpster, maybe his. It cost one tenant $60.00 for maintenance to take her couch, to recycling.

The tenant with the long time cancer problem is back, in the hospital again, with the same problem. He's scheduled to go to another hospital for test to find out if a specialist can do anything for him. To stop him from continuing to have to go, to the hospital. To be able to take nourishment as he's lost more then 100 lbs. and he is skin and bones now. He was getting better but had a relapse.

Well it's about the end of the month and tenants are moving out of their family unit. Another descent tenant will be gone. Lets see what they let move in. So now there's 4 family units vacant.

Here we go again. The maintenance man took that same tenant grocery shopping, in the company van. He even carried her groceries back to her unit. Not part of his job.

The tenant with those kids has been trying to get pain pills from two different other tenants. They both said no. So he pretended that he fell out of his car, onto the sidewalk. So he could call the ambulance and get pain pills at the hospital and a prescription. He must be smoking the marijuana he's been trying to sell. As he's been seen outside all glassy eyed and staring like he wasn't there. So he's smoking it himself. Both the marijuana and cigarettes inside his unit in violation of the owners no smoking rule in units.

Now that we have snow and colder. I'll wait and see if now they will still improve the parking area. They said they would do it no matter what the weather. Also the owners said they were going to pressure wash the building, to remove mold and more after the first frost. We have had several frosts but no pressure wash yet.

Early this morning there was a small doe, outside my window, feeding on plants.

Now there's deep holes, in the driveway. It needs to be fixed before someone has an accident. Especially if it gets covered with snow. Someone may not know the holes are there.

Things are to quiet here now. I don't know if it's the cold weather or the snow that's keeping tenants in and quiet. It feels like the calm before the storm. Now we are getting freezing rain. It took away most of the snow. We are having mild weather for the end of December. With rain and wind that took away the last of the snow.

The tenant with those kids. Now says he has a so-called caregiver. He asked another tenant to cash a check for her. Because she has no bank account or ID. How does she get here without driving. She must have a driver's license. As much as he's had a foul mouth to that tenant she was nuts to do him any favors. The tenant deposited the check and gave her part of the money. She was lucky that the check did clear. He's pulled things on her before and he's a drug dealer. Since she cashed the check for the so-called caregiver. She has not been seen here. The tenant was promised $25.00 for cashing the check but she's never got it.

The tenant that's been fighting cancer is back in the hospital. He was there a week until they regulated his latest system to try to help him. He came home but looks like skin and bones.

The big nor'ester snow storm turned out to be no big deal. Now we are having rain changing to a mix. This will wipe out what little snow we have.

The owners have put out a letter that they are going to enforce their rule about no smoking in units and you must be 25 feet from any building to smoke. But no one comes around to check on it. So it's just the usual redirect with no performance. We understand next year, under new federal laws, that there will be no smoking anywhere, on the property.

The tenant that's selling marijuana always smoked inside and threw his butts out the window. Now he smokes the marijuana inside also.

There are so many more important things that need to be taken care of and enforced then the smoking ban.

Now we are having 50 mile an hour winds and a power outage. The wind ripped off my storm door and broke it into pieces.

The tenant that's been fighting cancer is back, in the hospital. This time his condition shows this looks like his end of life. All his friends here will miss him. Especially me as we always went fishing and hunting together and shared other interests. He spent 12 hours in emergency and is on major pain medicine and other through the IV.. So he will stay in the hospital until the end. He doesn't want to see anyone. Not even relatives.

It was decided that he would come home with hospice because his condition is terminal.

The local newspaper has an ad, from the owners, that they want to hire a property manager. I wonder if the new property manager has quit? So far about his first 3 months he has done nothing to improve or take care of problems here or even come around the property.

Now again tenants are leaving their garbage on the ground by the dumpster. Animals have gotten into it. Someone keeps leaving the side door wide open and animals could get into the dumpster again.

Now we have so much friction between tenants. This causes hard feelings between some tenants.

That drug dealer tenant just got full custody of his two kids. We are all hoping that the owners will move him up to a family unit and away from our area. These units are not family units. They are senior and disability units.

The Tenants Assoc. has notified the property manager of his constant violations of a multitude of the owners rules. Also demanded that they do their job and get him out of our area.

The maintenance man constantly uses the company van for his own personal use. Even on weekends when even he's not working. He has been seen on weekends using the van to take his kids, to play baseball, at an area field.

There is always incidents going on here. Tenants tell other tenants what has happened and then tell another tenant a totally different story. So this makes a tenant mad at another tenant for no reason at all. This goes on here daily which makes so much bad feelings between tenants. I so much would like to get out of here. But financially I can't. So I'm stuck with all this.

The tenant that's been fighting cancer for so long. He's back, in his unit, in a hospital bed. Hospice nurse comes every day to see him. He's on a pain pump that puts pain medication, on a scheduled time program.

The letter that was sent, to the property manager, about the problems with that drug dealer tenant. Instead of him coming or at least sending the tenant a letter about the complaints. He sent the maintenance man to talk to the tenant about the complaints. That's not his job and it shows our new property manager is worthless, if he can't even confront a tenant that's violating the owners rules all the time. The property manager has not been seen on property in months. That tenant has ignored what was said to him. He is still continuing to violate the rules.

Refer to page 33 where the tenant cashed the check for the other tenants so-called caregiver. The state police just called the tenant, who cashed the check, and told her the check was fraudulent. She had to go, to the state police barracks and try to identify the woman she cashed the check for. I'm sure that other tenant got a cut, of the money. The woman got $100.00 and when the check cleared she gave the drug dealer the other $140.00 and he just pocketed it as his cut and she never got the $25.00 for cashing the check. She did identify the woman and may be summoned to testify in court. She also told the police that tenant is a drug dealer. Maybe the state police will come and investigate the drug dealer. Well this all may finally get him out of the complex.

The maintenance man said the owners know all about it and comes the inspection he will be out of here.

The tenant with cancer, his wife posted a note, on the door, no visitors. So we all know his time is short. Early on a Saturday morning he past away. Service came at 2 am and took him away. She says she will stay here, in the unit.

We had a major snow storm. This time I preempted leaving a message for the new property manager. The state and federal fire safety laws require the owners to provide two exits, in case of fire. The service needs to snow blow a path, at the rear entrances so tenants could get out in case of fire. They were here and snow blowed the sidewalks and came back later and plowed out the parking areas and snow blowed the path, at rear doors.

Now we have mild temperatures and all that snow is gone.

We just had our yearly unit inspections, to show we are keeping up our unit and any repairs needed. I was told that after this inspection the drug dealer will be out of the complex. I hope so but the owners have never followed through with anything.

It's been about 8 weeks since the wind storm ripped off my back storm door. So far they have not replaced it. This is the typical slow response, by the owners to anything needed done here.

I see the ambulance going out with lights flashing. It appears they took the drug dealer, to the hospital. Several times before he faked falling so he could go, to the hospital and get pain pills.

The owners showed up for a surprise inspection of random units. They are in violation of the owners rules and HUD's rules. Owners rules say a 48 hour written notice for entry and HUD's rules say a reasonable written notice in advance. I don't know if they went into my unit, as I was gone.

The drug dealer is back with a fractured leg. His whole right leg is in a cast. He put a picture of it on facebook. It looks like he faked another fall and being 100 lbs. overweight he fractured his leg. Others say he fractured his leg on purpose so he won't be evicted. He did this to his lower leg once before, when he tried to fake a fall. Because he owed 4 months back rent. Then it gave him time to sell enough drugs to pay off the back rent.

Here it is mid March and after the warmest winter since 1894. We now have cold weather and 20+ inches of snow, from the storm. This time the service did come and snow blow a path, at our rear entrances without tenants calling about it.

Now we have been notified of HUD's unit inspection. It will be random. The notice said they will enter 5 of the 24 units. So it's another big joke. We all hope they go into the drug dealer's unit. This might get him evicted. Previously the property managers have steered HUD away from problem units so they look good. This HUD inspection was the biggest joke of all. I don't know how many family units they went into. But they only went into one of the 12 units in the section I live in.

Now we are having mixed weather. Start as snow and inbetween rain showers. This just turns everything to ice. Also this cuts off the signal, on dish, so no tv. They say we are going to have this kind of weather, for a week.

Snow storm again. Heavy wet snow. This will end up as the snowiest March on record. The snow storms are continuing into April.

That drug dealer is going around to other tenants who he knows gets a prescription for pain pills and trying to buy some from them.

Now a mild week with rain storms. Between rain and snow melt there will be flooding.

The maintenance man came and went down to that same tenants unit. This time he brought her a bottle of alcohol as seen by me and another tenant.

Now today is the opening day of fishing. With all the rain we got the rivers are to high and also it's snowing again. In two days it's going to be 70 degrees.

Early Sunday morning a red fox ran along the sidewalk across from my back door.

The maintenance man is at it again. He only came to the complex to take that same tenant to do her personnel errands. Not to do any work here. When there's lots of things needing repairs, in the complex.

In one of the family units the husband left. Now the woman is having a lot of other people staying there with kids. The owners know nothing about what really goes on here. That's why tenants do these things. She said that her husband left because she would rather be with another woman.

They are redoing the siding on family units. When a lot of the siding, on the 12 senior units need to be done. Some siding is broken, holes and coming loose. Also the sides of the buildings that don't get sun are moldy. Seven months ago they said they are going to pressure wash our buildings. Still no sign of anything happening, as usual.

The visiting nurse came to check on the drug dealer, but was not home, as he has a fractured leg. She said that he is very close to be evicted, out of here. But we all have heard this before and nothing was done.

Now it's been 12 weeks since the wind ripped off my rear storm door and still they haven't replaced it. I've asked about it several times, nothing.

I've learned that several people have turned in that drug dealer to DCF for his treatment of his two young boys. Everyone hears his constant yelling and swearing, at the boys. Even late at night his neighbor hears all this. He's violent and has punched holes in the walls and broken a window three times. He also always owes back rent. When outside he lets the boys run loose with no supervision.

Today I was sitting outside with a neighbor. When a woman from SRS came, to that drug dealer's unit. We both could hear him yell you have to prove it. SRS was there quit a long time. Maybe this will wake him up and he will stop doing all his crap. But we hope they will take the kids away from him. This just might get him out of here. On the news SRS says they have more then 1300 kids in their care. Mostly due to the increase in drug use. He still smokes inside his unit in violation of the owners rules plus marijuana. They have not done anything about it. He continues to yall and swear, at his kids, half the night and keeps his neighbor from getting any sleep.

My neighbor, whose in a wheelchair, I've been taking her to doctors appointments and other places. She reimburses me for gas only. When she used this expense to lower her rent, they tried to tell me that it was income for me and tried to raise my rent. I said no and quoted from HUD's rules that it's not income. As a fact HUD's rules says reimbursement for transportation is not counted as income.

My neighbor and I was sitting outside and we saw car after car make a 3 minute stop at the drug dealers unit. It was obvious it was drug buys. My neighbor showed me a text from the drug dealer threating her and me and saying a tenant in a family unit said we were bad mouthing him. The tenant said he never told him anything and his wife said she still has his treating text to her on her cell phone.

I notified the owners about all this and it's time to bring the police in on it. According to the owners rules that threating text makes him subject to eviction. He has also violated 5 rules under criminal activity which any one violation is subject to eviction.

Sunday the drug dealer tried to start a confitation with 3 tenants.

Now the owners have let a woman with 4 kids and no job and no car. Move into a 2 bedroom family unit. The woman has a bed in the dining area, to sleep on. This should not be. We don't know if they told the owners the truth about who will be living there.

My neighbor is back seeing that drug dealer that left the valley to avoid being arrested. He's trying to get an apartment here or in the other complex. Property manager has been notified he's a drug dealer and has a criminal record.

Finally they are installing surveillance cameras to check on who comes an goes. Also to catch people coming in just to throw their garbage, in our dumpster. I told them to point one camera towards the unit the drug dealers in. Then they will have proof of his drug deals and maybe he will be gone. When he saw the cameras he asked the maintenance man if there are any units for rent elsewhere. Either he will be caught or have to stop selling drugs. Then he won't have that money, to pay his rent, and be evicted.

Now the surveillance cameras are working. They have already shown several cars coming to the drug dealers unit. It picks up the license plates. When shows multiple days of the same cars coming the police will be waiting for the cars with a search warrant then the owners can go to court and get an eviction and he will have to be out in 3 days. Unless the police arrest him before that.

Someone new moved into a family unit. Now we have kids everywhere. Little kids in the driveway with no adults in site. Now one of the kids has head lice and still running outside with other kids.

When the owners tried to raise my rent, the woman who called me was rude and arrogant about it. Even when I quoted HUD's rules in my favor. She's making up her own rules and never checked with Hud. I contacted HUD about it and they referred me to the State Housing Authority. The head, of the housing authority, sent me an e-mail stating I was correct and my reimbursement, for gas only, from a handicapped tenant, I take to medical appointments. When the tenant called the owners about it as a legitimate deduction, for her. That woman was rude to her, even after she read her the e-mail. She said it let me, off the hook, but would not except it as a medical deduction, for the tenant, to help lower an excessive increase in her rent. I wrote a letter to the property manager about all this.

Saturday night one tenant said cars were coming in and going a few minutes to that drug dealers unit. She could tell by all the headlights. Showing the comings and goings.

Here it is the second week in May and they still have not replaced my rear storm door that blew off and broke up in January. Everytime I asked about it I always got a phony excuse. That's how they take care of this place always.

The woman that moved in with 4 kids. Now a man has moved in with her. I'm sure she didn't tell the owners. But it's all on camera. His comings and goings.

The drug dealer is constantly yelling, at his kids, and at a lot of the tenants, for no reason. In the owners own rules he can be evicted for rule V, any other activity which impairs the physical or social environment of the premises. Plus 5 rules he has also violated. Anyone is subject to eviction.

Kids from the family units are riding up and down our sidewalks. They are not suppose to be down here. Kids going into the old chicken coop which is full of mold. Also the same kids are climbing all over the dumpster and even on top of it. All caught on camera.

At 8:30 pm on Saturday three kids were climbing on a play slide. They tipped it over and were banging on it and rolling it. I went out and yelled at them. There father was sitting at his front door [the drug dealer].

Then he yelled at them to stop and tip it up and apologize to me. If I had not gone out he would have let them continue. Two days before he ran his filthy mouth to me and my neighbor. Now he's trying to be Mr. Nice Guy. Earlier he apologized to me and my neighbor for his activities. He must have gotten a possible eviction notice. Either by mail or a phone call, by the property manager.

At this time of night a 4 year old girl was riding a tricycle in the driveway with no adult insight. I found out the mother went away and left a 11 year old to take care of the 4 year old.

Monday those new kids, three of them ganged up on another kid and hit him in the side of the head, with a rock. None of those new kids never have supervision. The father, of the kid that was hit had a yelling confiltation with the mother. Then the EMTs came, then two sheriffs cars and the ambulance came. Treated the boy and all left. Then two state police cars came. After they left two other state police cars came, to talk to the father and tried to talk to the mother of the kids. They gave the father, of the kid hit, a summons to appear in court for harassment.

Last year the mother of the drug dealer was caught on a store camera stealing a donation can for meals on wheels for seniors. Now today, on facebook was a picture of the same woman caught on a store camera stealing two donation cans.

The property manager was here to review the surveillance tapes on what went on and was reported to them. My neighbor and I gave him an earful about more things going on. He is going to talk to all involved but he says he won't be able to get them out of here. That's a bunch of crap. There own rules give them the right to evict all involved.

They finally replaced my storm door that blew off in January and broke. It only took them 4 months to get around to replacing it.

My neighbor called me that those new tenants, in a family unit were making fun of the drug dealer, whose in a wheelchair. This is just retaliation for his yelling argument with them. I told the neighbor tell him it's harassment and call the police. All the filthy remarks he has made to everyone. We are glad. It's just payback for his filthy remarks and e-mail threats to tenants. His kids and some from a family unit had pulled out garbage, from the dumpster, and threw it all over.

After the property manager reviewed the tapes. From the surveillance cameras. He had a long talk with the new tenant with 4 kids. So far it's been quiet. Then there was two men here who also looked at the tapes. They talked to several. In the family units.

The drug dealer had another yelling fight with tenants in a family unit. State police were called.

Memorial evening kids running loose and yelling with no adult supervision.

Here's another day where the maintenance man came only to take that same tenant, to the drug store, in the company van. Last night the drug dealers kids and two other kids were using a slide to climb a tree and hang on the branches and banging, on the slide and stand. With no adults around. Now they are doing it every night.

A neighbor just went into the drug dealers unit and bought a bag of marijuana for $40.00. She said he had a big bag of it on the table. Shortly afterwards we saw two tenants from a family unit came down, to his unit, for a buy.

When I came home Saturday there was a car parked in my spot. I drove into the field and came nose to nose with the car. There was one guy in it with music blaring and the driver was in the drug dealers unit, making a buy. I heard the drug dealer say wait till I go in. So I would not see who it was. Then they left right away.

That drug dealer is openly causing trouble between tenants. Making remarks, about another tenant, so everyone hears it

There's still no sign that the owners are doing anything about him.

Here we go again. This time up at the family units. One of the boys, who has mental problems. Had a cat, by the tail, and was flinging it around and tossing it. Another neighbor had an argument, with the mother, over it and she should be a mother. All ensued with yelling. Then the mother left, with her live-in girlfriend, to a gay pride goings on, for 4 days. She left her 13 year old daughter incharge of her brother, who was throwing the cat.

Multiple tenants called the property manager to review the surveillance tapes end then come here for a meeting with tenants. The property manager called and basically said he can't do anything. That's because he's changing the owners rules without an addendum, to tenants, with the changes. He didn't even know the rules his boss had put out years ago. These latest incidents violated three of the owners rules. Any one which makes the tenant subject to eviction. He is ignoring all this and making his own rules.

With all this crap going on here and the property manager doing nothing about it. Now the kids, from the family units, are coming into our area and making noise and riding their bikes up and down our sidewalks. Also climbing trees and hanging, on the branches, with no adult supervision. Now 4 tenants, including myself, have had enough and trying to find another place to move to. When this was brought up to the manager he said move if you don't like it. He refused to do anything about all the problems, including the drug dealers living here. He keeps changing the rules, that have been in effect, since I've been here, 8 years. The important things that need to be taken care of he looks the other way and does nothing. He has proved to everyone that he is worthless. Just like all the previous property managers.

My neighbor tells me that the drug dealer is putting extreme filth on facebook. The tenant is sick, in the head. He has often, in the past, acted crazy and threatened other tenants. The property manager has been told all this, in the past, several times by multiple tenants. Still he has done nothing.

At 7pm there was at least 6 kids, from the family units, climbing the tree, outside my front door. Two of them, one with a bat the other with a plastic sword, banging on the bushes outside my bedroom window. One was against my front door. I went out and asked them twice to go home. They just ignored me until I yelled it at them. Then they left and I could see that their mothers were sitting right out front of their units. I called and left a message, on the manager's phone, about all this and do something.

This afternoon those kids pelted my car windshield with eggs. I reported it and took a picture with my cellphone. After 7 pm I saw 10 kids over at the dumpster pulling stuff out. The next morning I went out and cut the lower limbs off that tree so they can't climb it.

People who don't live in public housing can not imagine what goes on. Now one tenant is causing major problems and fights with other tenants. The woman is totally sick in the head. She's headed for another nervous breakdown. With her insane ramblings she has alienated everyone and no one is going to have anything to do with her. Especially me as she's saying things about my good friend, who past away this year. What she's saying is not true. She is leaving me strange messages on my answering machine. One of the messages could be considered a threat that she may try to cause me trouble. The visiting nurse is going to contact her son about all this. She needs professional help. The nurse saw this when she visited her and talked to others. Her son came and picked her up and she's going to be gone two weeks. I also found out that she has been in the hospital mental ward twice. Once for three months.

Now there's so many skunks around. At least 5 have been seen. They are even out during the day. Often you can smell them in different areas. The maintenance man said if I see any skunks go ahead and shoot them.

Well the drug dealer is feeling retaliation, from those kids. They left nails by his car. Now they threw rocks and made chips, in several places, on his windshield. That should be on the surveillance cameras. Also we saw a woman come to the unit where there's 4 trouble making kids live. We hope it was DCF. Another step in getting rid of them.

Further, the drug dealer says now there's lots of scrapes, on his car. That's just some payback by those kids, good.

Things have been quiet, for awhile. But we never count on it. The drug dealer showed up, on Saturday, towing a piece of junk camper. He parked it in front of his door. Ot has out of state plates, no electric hookup for lights or electric brakes. Someone gave it to him and paid him $100.00 to take it away. He said he was taking it up to his mothers on Sunday. Next thing he said it would be here 2 days. Later he said it would be here 4 days. The rules say he can't have it here even one day.

This was all reported, to the property manager. By me and others. He called me back and said he talked, to the tenant. The tenant claims he has someone to take it and it will be gone soon.

The drug dealer cut the bush, by his front door, to the ground. Without permission or even asking the owners. His kids throw food, in the bush.

The property manager was here. He said the woman, with the 4 kids, who he gave an eviction notice to. If the kids are quite and not making trouble, like they have been doing, that he's given them a second chance, to stay here.

Well it's Friday afternoon and there's two state troopers here. They are talking with tenants up at the family units. Both tenants got a summons to appear in court, for disorderly conduct. They are the two that received eviction notices.

Well here we go again. Its Thursday morning and a tenant went over to the drug dealer's unit. To complain to him about all the noise all hours, coming from his unit. Also his yelling and swearing at his two kids. He did nothing but scream, yell and swear, at the tenant. Over and over again. Then he came outside and started yelling, swearing and threatening myself and a tenant I was talking to. We had nothing to do with what went on. At least four of us called the property manager and lodged a major complaint. I left a stinging complaint and demanded he do something today, about it. And get him out of here. Friday he again threatened the tenant he threatened the day before.

The property manager called a tenant, in the family unit, and asked him if he wants to be in charge of neighborhood watch. He said yes only if I'm part of the watch. I said yes but we need to find out our authority and what we can do and what we can't do. Also make sure that the owners will back us up and not their usual way of not following through.

The property manager was here and denied he asked us to be in neighborhood watch. Also he never addressed the problems here that multiple tenants have been complaining about.

So I've sent info to HUD and other agencys, including the governor and the newspaper. Let them know the problems and I have documented info on all that has gone on.

Finally we had a blow-out meeting with the property manager, a mediator, myself, three other tenants and the drug dealer. Everything was discussed from the problems with the drug dealer, his yelling, swearing and threatening of other tenants. With the problems with kids causing problems and running loose with no adults around. To maintenance, landscaping and more the owners are not doing. We want the drug dealer evicted. I showed the property manager 5 of their own rules which any one of them they can evict him. He has violated these 5 rules over and over again. I gave him 4 pages of documentation of his violations. The owners won't even try to evict him.

So I asked for federal help. I sent a letter to HUD with copies to the housing authority, DCF, the governor and the news paper. Also a separate letter to the fire marshal as the drug dealer uses his grill at his front door and against the building. In violation of fire safety and the owner's rules that grills must be 20 feet from the building.

All in all I will be very surprised if the owners do anything. They have a past record of doing nothing.

The property manager said he would come and go around with me so I can show him what's needed, to be done.

The drug dealer is having a bbq fund raiser for himself. To repair his apartment, get a better car and a new wheelchair. He won't spend the money on these things. He will pocket the money. The fund raiser is in another town where the majority of the residents are low-lifes like him.

Today the lawn mowing service came and mowed and weed wacked. Except they didn't bother to weedwack at my neighbors back door area. I cut the weeds myself, for her.

It's been 6 days since the meeting and no sign of the property manager coming to look at things needed, to be done here. Also no sign of the sheriff coming to talk to two of us, to be neighborhood watch.

The woman in the family unit with the four kids who have been causing problems. Now her neighbor says she is pregnant and there is no man living with her.

Tenant in the family unit was evicted and was to be out of here 15 days ago, but is still here.

Upcoming week is wet weather all week. So this will give the property manager an excuse not to come this week and look at what needs to be done here.

The trap the maintenance man set has caught several skunks. He needs to catch the big white skunk. It maybe living in the load storage shack, which needs to be torn down.

I hope HUD and the state agency are investigating the owners as per letters from the Tenants Assoc.

There's a sign on the command room that no one under a certain age is allowed in there without an adult. Also the door is to be kept locked. Later that day several kids went in without an adult. I headed that way and one kid outside I heard him yell, to them, watch out. I heard them close and lock the door. I unlocked it and they locked it back up. I unlocked it and held my key so they can't lock it again. I said read the sign you are not supposed to be in here. They left and I locked the door.

The drug dealer is playing his game. When ever I come out I hear him yell, at the kids, I told you to pick up that. I told you not to be doing that.

This early morning I looked out my back door and a large black and white skunk was walking along near the building.

The drug dealer is sucking up to tenants. We all hope it is because either the owners are finally doing something or the letters the Tenants Assoc. sent have come down on him and the owners.

The property manager left me a message that someone from the sheriff's office will come to talk to us about the neighborhood watch. But not until October. That's a month away. Why wait?

The drug dealer was driving around with a 3 year old in the front seat and hanging out the window, of his car. He's watching the girl for another tenant.

Again tenants are telling something to another tenant and they elaborate and tell another tenant. Then that makes problems between other tenants. This is the kind of thing that goes on in low income complexes. That's why there's so much tension and aggravation here. People always find a reason to spread rumors that escalate and mostly turn out to be untrue.

It's Sunday afternoon and everyone can here the drug dealer yelling and screaming at his kids. Monday the lawn mowing service was here. His kids leave all kinds of crap all over the lawn. The big stuff the guy mowing has to stop and pick up and put it out of his way. All the other stuff, paper, chip bags and other plastic containers just get mowed and chewed up all over.

The state police was here today. They were looking for a tenant in a family unit for his kid breaking into the mail boxes and destroying mail.

The drug dealer has kept both his kids home from school for two days. But they are not sick. They both are out running around and riding their bikes.

Well the property manager came back for a meeting with others, from the owners. We went over all that needs to be done from repairs, maintenance, landscaping etc. They said they will be getting things done soon. But already the time frame for doing everything has been pushed back. We just have to wait and see what goes, no choice.

One tenant has been waiting almost a year for her back broken storm door to be replaced. But instead they replaced the drug dealers storm door that he broke a short time ago.

A neighbor just bought plants, in a pot. Kids smashed the pot and put the plant on the hood of her car.

Kids that the drug dealer is suppose to be watching were running all over, with him not insight. His kids throw crap all over the common area.

Friday finally landscapers came. Just in one day this place looks 100% better. There's more work to be done. They will be back. The owner's man didn't show up so I showed the landscapers what needed to be done. Typical of the owners.

Friday afternoon the kids were sitting in a baby stroller and coming down the bank and close to the parked cars, with no adults insight.

Today finally they came and graded the driveway. It's been in dangerous condition all summer.

A tenant asked the maintenance man to tell the drug dealer to clean up his mess, by the back door. He told her if she doesn't like to look at it, sit out back. Just what I've been saying they act like they are afraid of him. It also shows the owners are totally worthless.

A paving company came and are putting a new layer of asphalt over the old broken asphalt private road. But are not going to do any paving on our driveway or the road through the property. But by just slapping another layer on an old broken road is wrong. Next year they will have to repair it. Also they were supposed to raise the road and crown it so the rain water didn't run on it and freeze. They did not even spray an oil base before paving. I can see all this because I worked on highway construction for years.

Friday the landscapers came back but were only here a half of a day. They left a lot more to still do.

Now they said they were going to pressure wash the mold off of our siding. This is the 4th year they told us that and nothing was ever done.

The property manager is harassing a decent tenant because of her financial situation. She has trouble paying one months rent. He lets the drug dealer slide for several months until he sells drugs and pays his back rent. The owners have never sent the tenant the paperwork with her new rent. She has to sign it that she accepts the new rent. Just another situation that shows the property manager is worthless and acts afraid of the drug dealer. A church group paid her rent.

Three kids, at the family units, are throwing rocks onto the roof. With no adults around. Then 6 kids with 3 of them under 5 years old riding bikes in the driveway and on the steep banks and still no adults around to see anything. Kids leave bikes and all kinds of things all over the common area and along the driveway.

Four kids on the side of the driveway jumping over things and more with not one adult insight, on the property. The sheriff's car came in and stopped and he was taking the kids names. Maybe DCF asked the sheriff to check the goings on here.

It's Friday again and the landscapers are here. This time they brought a cherry picker. So they can do the high stuff. Still left a lot to do. Seems like they only are going to come on Fridays.

Again the drug dealer is having a verbal argument with a woman tenant from the family unit, out in the driveway.

Once again the drug dealer's kids bent the light post over.

This Friday some showers and the landscapers never came. I wonder if they are not coming anymore.

It's Tuesday and the workers are here putting up a fill rain gutter system with downspouts, front and back of our 12 units.

The constant stress from some tenants and the owners ignoring all this and contributing to this with one of their office employees. With her rude and arrogant attitude to anyone who calls her. This all has forced one tenant to move, for her health, before all this causes her more health problems.

The drug dealer now tells he's moving. This is the 4th time he said he was moving. He has told different tenants a different town he's moving to. So he may not be moving again.

The maintenance man was here. A tenant asked him to put in a new bulb, in the bathroom. He said he didn't have his van with supplies. She told him to go to the hardware store and get a bulb. He said he didn't have his wallet, but he had the nerve to ask the tenant to borrow money to get a beer, on his way home. She said no. I went and took a bulb out of the common room bathroom and put in for her.

I came home about 5:30 pm and there was 6 little kids, in the driveway. Running up and down, on their bikes. With no adults in sight anywhere. Also all kinds of junk along the driveway everywhere.

The drug dealer told me today he's moving November 1st. We will all be happy.

The property manager has told tenants that beginning in 2018 that HUD's rule says no smoking anywhere, on the property. That's a lie. HUD's web sight says they passed the rule in 2017 and all of the properties, under HUD, must comply by July of 2018. The rule says tenants must smoke 25 feet from any building, not the entire property. The property manager posted the 25 foot rule sign in our 12 unit area, but exempted the 12 family units. He can't do this so he's in violation of HUD's rule.

Ambulance was here today. Up at a family unit but they didn't take anyone, to the hospital.

A tenant, in a family unit, his dog bit a neighbors kid.

My neighbor lost her set of keys, in the driveway. We looked but could not find them. It's her car keys, door key, mail box key and her gas cap key.

Then a couple of nights later someone was seen going through her van and accidently set off the alarm. Then a neighbor heard it and says he saw someone, in the van. She called the state police and they took her report, but said they can't do anything unless they steal the van. She called the property manager and asked him to review the surveillance tapes. But as usual he's out of the office. It took him weeks before he looked at the tapes. He said nothing showed and the cameras don't work at night.

I stayed up late and was armed. To keep an eye on her van. There was two suspicious signs, I checked out, but found nothing. When I got up the next day her van was still here. She let everyone know if anyone finds her keys she will give them a reward, no questions asked.

After they put up a complete gutter system, no one came and cleaned out leaves. Now it's raining and some of the downspouts are not running water. That's because they are packed with leaves. I cleaned out the by my unit. Then water came out.

The tenant who lost her keys, they were found in the bushes. So who ever went through her van and set off the alarm panicked and through them away.

They finally fixed my parking area by raising it some and put down stay mat and compacted it. But everything else they said they were going to do never happened.

It's Saturday at about 4pm and the maintenance man just showed up, in the company van, only to bring that same tenant something he picked up for her. He doesn't work weekends.

November 1st has come and gone and the drug dealer is still here. If the owner of the place he was to rent checked his rent history here, he would not get the place. He said the deal fell through but he's moving to another place the middle of this month.

The tenant that's been fighting, with the owners over her rent she doesn't owe. Her daughter lives in the family unit and her rent varies depending her changing monthly income. It's obvious her charges are mixed up with her daughter's rent. So finally there is going to be a meeting with the owners. I am going to the meeting with her so they don't walk all over her like they have been doing.

Today two pickup trucks were loading furniture and more from the drug dealer's unit. He's moving out and everyone, in the complex is happy he's gone. He stole a power cord, from a neighbor's electric chair, to charge his and took it with him. He trashed his apartment and it reeks of the smell of urine. It will take several thousand dollars to repair the unit and get the smell out.

The property manager called the drug dealer about the cord. He said it was his and he's not giving to her. The neighbor called the state police and reported everything. A state trooper called me for my report as I witnessed his kids getting the cord and bringing it to him. He was sitting in his car with the engine running and when the kids handed him the cord and got into the car he left. So he stole it. He had his kids tell the neighbor he just needed to borrow it for an hour to charge his chair, a lie and he didn't have the nerve to do it himself. The trooper called my neighbor back and said with my statement they have enough to arrest him. A trooper will come here and take our statements. Two other tenants had seen that he tore up his cord. He had also when he tore up his cord.

Now the drug dealer called the tenant and told her he just found the cord, in his car, and will bring it to her in two days. He was going to call the state police and tell them that. The state police had called him about the cord. So once again he commits crime and may get away with it. My neighbor just called me to tell me a state trooper called her and he's coming to take our statements. After the trooper got back, to the office, he called the tenant and told her they are bringing him in for a statement but they have enough evidence to charge him with theft.

The drug dealer keeps calling the tenant but she doesn't answer the phone. The state police said have no contact with him or any of his family. He's most likely trying to get her to drop the charges. She says she's not going to drop the charges. The state police said she can't drop the charges. The drug dealer's grandmother came and brought her charging cord back. He didn't have the nerve to come and face anyone. We both may have to go to court, to testify.

All the times the police have been to his unit now has caught up with him.

A tenant said his facebook sight all the new things he has bought. So he has money to pay for the repairs that he trashed in the unit. The new bikes he bought his kids this summer are behind the dumpster.

The drug dealer called a tenant and was bent out of shape and told the tenant he was going to return the cord. Why all this with the police. He thought he was going to get away with stealing the power cord. He didn't expect the owner to contact the police or there was a collaborating witness, myself.

Sunday the neighbor heard someone in the drug dealer's former unit. Another tenant saw the woman, from a family unit, come down with one of her kids. They came back with arms full of items, from the unit and took it back to their unit.

Thanksgiving evening we see the ambulance is up at a family unit.

A tenant tried to clean the snow off her dish, for tv, she fell. The ambulance came and took her to the hospital. She came home and her arm is broken in two places.

The maintenance man went down to that same tenant's apartment and just wanted to come in with no notice. She said no you just can't walk in. Then he said he didn't have his wallet and wanted to borrow $10.00, from her, to buy beer on the way home. She said no. The owners need to realize he's not doing his job properly and this is not the first time he tried to borrow money from her, to buy beer. According to the owner's rules when you put in a work order. Maintenance is required to take care of the problem within 10 days. This never happens. Always way much longer or never. Some tenants have been waiting a year or more to have their storm door replaced. When my door blew off in a storm in January and busted up, it was 6 months before I got a new one. There are new doors on sight, in the boiler room, still in there boxes.

Now they have started to redo the drug dealer's unit. Thursday the state police were at the unit. The maintenance man called them and handed the police a bag. He must have found the drug dealer's stash. Earlier a tenant saw the woman, with 4 kids, come out of his unit, trying to hide a bag. It must have been more of his drugs. Because she hangs around with a tenant that used to come down and get high, with the drug dealer. So he probably knew where the drugs were stashed. Hopefully with the discovery, of the drugs, this will bring more down on the drug dealer, then just stealing the tenants power cord, for her wheelchair.

The property manager has been informed about all this from the Tenant's Assoc.

The property manager told me that he is trying to evict the woman with 4 kids and she is pregnant. Maybe with her latest actions that will be enough to get her evicted.

I hope this wakes up the owners to do a better background check on new possible tenants, we hope.

I've learned something today. But it's all second hand information. The drug dealer never left this town. All the different places he told people he was moving to, was a lie. He's living in a house across from the trailer park. He's in a house that the owner is in jail, his drug supplier.

The same tenant, this information came from, says the maintenance man has been making advances to her and she doesn't want him to come to her unit.

With this below zero temperature the other building, with six units, the boiler went. But the owners never notified the tenants as to what's happening, no heat.

Now having real cold weather. Car would not start. Had to borrow a battery charger. It took awhile but it started ok. Need to run it more to keep up the battery charge. More real cold weather coming and snow afterwards.

We now have deep snow and according to the state and federal fire safety laws the owners must provide two exits incase of fire. We have elderly tenants and one in a wheelchair. As usual the owners have not cleared an exit path, through the snow, at the back doors of the 12 units. This has happened to many times. Finally they came back and snowblowed a path. Now it's warm and heavy rain. Then it turned colder and ice.

The property manager still has not learned to do his job. He still acts like the social worker he was. His job is to look out for the wellbeing of the tenants. He does the opposite. People coming in here that don't live here have more rights then we do. Such as, there's very limited parking for tenants, yet he said they can park in my space that I've used for over 8 years, and that I have to find another place to park. Numerous times I've come home and there's someone parked in my space. So I park behind them and lock my car. He say if I do they can have my car towed away. With all the snow I shovel out my space myself and why should someone use it, especially a non resident. I asked for a sign for resident parking only. He said they don't do that. But another area has signs for resident parking only.

They put out a letter to all tenants as of a certain date any vehicle that is unregistered or no current inspection sticker, will be towed away. One tenant's van is unregistered because right now she doesn't have the money, to register it. It is expired 2+ months. But they told her the letter was not meant for her, so forget about it. Then why did they even give her a notice. Now they put off towing cars for two weeks.

This is the way the manager has run things. What's ok for some tenants is not ok for others. Such as HUDs smoking rule. You must be 25 feet from the building. He put up signs for our 12 units but told the ones in the family units they didn't have to be 25 feet from the building. HUDs rule applies to the whole complex, not just where the manager says. I read HUD's rule on their web sight. It is for the entire complex.

We now have 10+ inches of new snow. The service was here, with a snowblower, to clear the sidewalks. But again they didn't clear a path at the back doors as required by fire safety laws.

The driveway and all the area here is share ice. Yet they didn't sand anywhere. Sun softened the ice which made big ruts from cars driving through. The next day the ruts were frozen. Making driving dangerous.

Now we have an upcoming unit inspection, by the owners. Each year it gets later and later. Started out in late November and now this one is late February. This is part of the recertification, of the tenants, to live here. The manager spent about 3 minutes in each unit.

Monday there was someone working in the boiler room where the other 6 units get their heat and hot water from. Tuesday they had no heat. Over 24 hour period the heat went out 4 times. Before finally fixed.

Now it's 70 degrees and rain. The driveway is deep mud ruts. Now cold again and those ruts froze and making driving dangerous again.

The maintenance man is showing up unannounced to do miner repairs in units. That was found during inspection. With no work orders and annoying one of the tenants. He showed up at my unit when I came home and asked me if it's ok to fix the tub drain. He knows better as I told him before never go into my unit unless I'm home. Because if he did I'd get him fired. Some of the things he's doing he should have been already fired. What he said he fixed in my unit still doesn't work. There's so much other repairs needed, in the complex, that he has work orders for. But he's not doing them. Instead he's doing goof off repairs. This is typical for him.

Also the maintenance man still making advances to that same tenant. She is very nervous when he comes, to her unit, no matter what for.

This am, in the field across from my front door. There was a big fox running around.

He maintenance man came back and to my surprise he actually got the tub drain to work.

Now another big snow storm. The service came to plow and snowblow the sidewalk. But again they didn't snowblow a path at the back doors as required by state and federal fire safety laws.

The morning after the big snow storm there was four doe outside my back door. They were feeding on the bushes.

We just had HUD's inspection. They went to two units out of the 12, in my area. Went to two units in the family section and they were gone. Another joke and a waste of time.

Another big snow storm. As usual the service never cleared the path at our back doors. As required by fire safety laws. Some tenant called and complained and they came back and cleared the path.

All the property manager's talk about towing away unregistered vehicles. There's a car parked at the family unit area with no license plate. He was here and had to see it. But did nothing about it.

It's late March and already skunks have been seen around the complex.

They finally finished repairing the unit the drug dealer trashed before he moved out. He was in a wheelchair and paralyzed from the waste down. From a car crash. So he had no control over body functions. If you walked by you chock on the smell of urine. It took 3 months to repair and replace toilet, bathtub, refrigerator, stove and floor.

First we had the owners inspection of every unit. The HUD's inspection of random units. Now we were notified that a state agency was going to have inspection of every unit over a 3 day period. That means tenants have to be home for 3 days. Because no tenant wants them in their unit unless they are home. One of the days is social security day when tenants have to go to the bank and take care of their bills. This way we don't know what days they will be here. They said they would only be, in a unit, 5-10 minutes. They could do all the units in a half of a day.

The first two inspections were a joke. Owners spent about 3 minutes in each unit. HUD's was a bigger joke. Now we will be subject to an even bigger joke by the state inspection.

New people moved into the former drug dealer's unit. Already we all see they are druggies. They are friends with a druggie from the family units. Who used to come down and get stoned with the drug dealer. They get rid of one problem and let another problem, for us, to move in. That again shows the property manager is worthless and doesn't care about the tenants.

Those new tenants are rejects from their other complex in the town. The tenants there all wanted them out of their complex.

The property manager has lost all friendship, respect and credibility from all tenants.

Within a few day period the ambulance came twice, to take a neighbor, to the hospital. She still doesn't look good.

Some tenants including myself are trying to find a better place to live. But the cost of rentals are so high no one can afford them on a social security check only.

It is such a shame that when you get to be a senior that you have to put up with all this crap.

Owners act like they don't even care. When you ask for help from any state, federal or political people you get nothing. At one time I tried to get help from our senator. I got nothing. He said he was for seniors, veterans and those in need. I told him I was all three. Do you think I got anything, no.

After all the work in that unit. Today maintenance brought a new stove, for the unit. They already replaced that. The owners are doing more for those rejects then they do for long time tenants that need things repaired or replaced, for a long time.

We were told the woman was bed ridden. A lie. She's sitting out back fully dressed and smoking. He's sitting in his car with the music blaring and smoking marijuana. All summer probably all his drug friends will be down here. All the tenants are so mad about them being here and mad at the property manager for letting them in here.

The latest inspection by a service was not a problem. They only went to a few units. Not everyone as the notice said. Also he took pictures of all the outside, including the roofs. The guy told me he will make a 20 year plan of what needs to be done here. Then it's up to the owners to get financing and decide what they are going to do an when.

The woman that's supposed to be bed ridden, she is walking all over the complex. So all that was a lie to let them move down here. Both of them were out back smoking marijuana.

The guy was parked at the beginning of our road. A car behind me stopped at his car and made a transfer of goods to him. Then he raced into here and up to his druggie pal's unit. That had to be a drug buy. That's what the drug dealer, that left here, always did. They think no one would know what they are doing.

Saturday am I see the new tenant's car is parked half on the sidewalk. He probably was high, on drugs, when he came home.

Monday afternoon they both went out in the car. She was driving. Another lie about her being bed ridden.

A tenant at the complex they came from said all day long she walked all over and rode the elevator up and down all day. So she's not bed ridden.

Today the maintenance man came and cleaned leaves out of the rain gutters. But only where there is a downspout. With all the rain coming it will wash the rest of the leaves to the downspouts. He should have cleaned all of the gutters. Typical half ass job.

Today I learned those new tenants came from the owners other complex in a lousy area full of low lifes. Then 6 months at the other complex, in this town, before they dumped them on us.

The property manager got a stinging letter from the Tenants Association with all these complaints. He was told he lost all friendship, reliability and credibility with all tenants, until he gets them out of our complex.

Facts are coming out about corruption in the owners office. The woman that figures rents is making up her own rules and not following the correct way of doing it. One tenant was told what her new rent was to be but never sent her the printout with the information and she was to sign accepting the new rent. But instead the owner's person raised the rent without notifying the tenant. Then when the tenant called to check on something she was told that she was not paying her full rent and owes money. That's illegal to do that and the tenant doesn't owe it.

It's a Tuesday afternoon in April. The maintenance man came only to sit out back with that same tenant, all afternoon. Not to do any work here. When there is so many things need to be done. A lot of repairs, clean up the areas and more. Instead of working he's goofing off here. The former tenant, up at the family units, drive in. He's not allowed on this property and he's driving with a criminally suspended drivers license. The maintenance man told the tenant to call the owners about it. He won't then they would know he's not working. Because he's not supposed to be here and he's not where he is supposed to be doing work.

Just learned the new tenant is mad. Because the owners called him about his smoking marijuana, in his car, out front of his unit. At least 6 tenants saw him. Because he had his radio blaring music. Good it's about time he got nailed. He complained the tenants at the owners other place, in town, were on him all the time. He should have never been put here. This area is seniors or ones with disability. They are neither. The two bedroom unit was handicap and they changed it for them. A big mistake. His neighbor says she smells an odor of marijuana coming from his unit. Owners rule as no smoking in units. Also possession of a controlled substance is subject for eviction. They both were fighting and yelling at each other. Disturbing their neighbor. By their side window there's lots of cigarette butts on the ground. So like their previous tenant they are smoking inside and tossing the butts out the window.

The property manager was here and all this was brought up to him. He went and knocked on the door. No one answered and the manager said no one home. I told him that 5 minutes ago I saw him come home. Instead of going back the manager left. Then they opened the windows to get the smoke out and air out the unit. There's never been a window open since they have been here.

There's a former tenant [family unit] who is on a court order not to be on the property. He's still driving although he just was arrested for driving with a criminal suspended license. He was on property all day, in and out, seeing his girlfriend. Maintenance man was here and had to see Jim but didn't report it. All this will be on the surveillance camera tapes. The manager was told all this.

It's a nice sunny warm may day. The grass is growing fast and the mowing service will be coming soon. The whole area is littered with branches, pine cones and leaves, from the winter.

The maintenance man comes all the way here, from where ever he was, and rakes up just the area behind that same tenant's back door and leaves.

A woman living in a family unit. Her boyfriend is a drug dealer and sells to the new tenant. I found out he's been selling drugs, to that tenant, when he lived in a city away from here.

Snakes are back there was a big one by my back door. Also two woodchucks and the maintenance man said he was not going to trap anything anymore. Woodchucks and skunks but I can go ahead and shoot them.

The new tenants neighbor called the property manager. Because the new tenants yell and swear and wake her up early. Also at night they do the same thing and annoy her. She told him that she put up with the drug dealer yelling, swearing and screaming, when he lived there. She's not going to do it again.

Saturday there was two state troopers here and at a tenant's unit, in the family section. I found out that those two tenants were caught on camera, at the local supermarket, stealing money and purse from an 80 year old shopper. The property manager was told about it. He said he was going to call the state police. Also this may be finally enough evidence to evict them.

The property manager was here today. He's waiting for the police report. So he can proceed to get them evicted. He said it could take a month to evict them out of here. Now there's a machine, at their unit, to kill all their bed bugs. I've been told this is the 3rd time they have had bed bugs. It may be spreading up at the family units. I saw a girl carry out a mattress and put it into the dumpster.

The so called bed ridden new tenant was driving the car by herself with no one else, in the car.

Memorial weekend a female tenant in a family unit was taken, to the hospital, by ambulance for an overdose on drugs. She's a crack attick. She has been seen back yet.

The same weekend another tenant, in a family unit, was stopped for an unregistered vehicle and also a stolen inspection sticker. Also no legal driver's license. He was stopped again by the state police in front of the local school. He had 3 little kids, in the car, and not one of the kids was in a required kids seat. He was seen coming home at 8 pm with his girlfriend driving behind him. So they took him in and she must have bailed him out.

The saga continues. There is a lesbian couple, in a family, unit that had a big verbal fight, outside. Yelling and swearing. One left with her bags and walked down the driveway. Not been seen since.

The new tenants, the guy has not been around for almost a week and no sign of his car. The woman, who is supposed to be bed ridden, is seen often driving a different car. The drug addict that lives at the other complex, in the area, brought him here just to deliver drugs to another tenant. They came back later and dropped the guy off here.

The maintenance man was here, with a trailer, to take away things left at the dumpster by tenants. He was asked to clean leaves, out of the gutters, as they didn't work during the rain storm. He denied that he was told about it. I was with the tenant that called the property manager about it and more, 4 days ago. He called the tenant back about it. Also during the storm a large tree came down, just missing a family unit, 5 days ago. It's still on the ground. A service came and cleaned up the downed tree and some of the standing tree left. Maintenance man finally came and is cleaning out the gutters. The property manager is here and I showed him why the downspouts were not working and the ends should be up on a splash block. He said he would ask the maintenance man about it because he knows nothing about construction. The maintenance man knows less about construction. Maintenance finally finished cleaning out the gutters and sprayed each unit, outside, to keep earwigs out. Kids climbing on top of the dumpster. No adults outside to watch these little kids of 4 and 5 years old.

The new tenant's father was here for a few days. He told another tenant that his son is not her care giver. He's her boyfriend and they sleep together. Then they lied to get into here and a 2 bedroom unit. The owner's again never did a check on them before letting them in here. He borrowed a bed for his father.

The drug dealer, that comes here often, went into the new tenant's unit, without knocking. So he was expected, for a drug delivery. This happens often.

Now the owners are having a preinspection for next months capital improvement's inspection. They say that they have to enter all units. That inspection before was for the outside, of the buildings and the structure. Not the inside. This preinspection is just so the owners can snoop on the decent tenants. They are afraid of the low-life and crud tenants. They keep letting them move in and ruin it for all the decent tenants.

In the 9 plus years I have been here the percentage of crud tenants, they have let in, has increased dramatically. Soon they will out number the good tenants. That's because the owners and especially the property manager are worthless.

I've learned that a tenant, in a family unit, who has been in trouble with the police before. He now has stolen jewelry and stolen guns, in his unit.

Now today is July 30th, 2018. This is the last day the owners have to put up HUD's smoking rules. Which is you must smoke 25 feet from any building. This rule applies to the entire complex. Not done. This makes the owner in violation of HUD's rules.

Someone shot off large fireworks only 10 feet from a family unit. They called the police, but no one showed up. They could have set the building on fire.

One of the woman tenants threw the maintenance man out of her unit. He comes and just walks in and has been aggressive towards her. He even tries to kiss her. She should report him and get him fired.

The state police were here and arrested a tenant, in a family unit, for beating up the woman. He's due to serve 6 months, for other crimes, and this will add to it. Also now in domestic violence the police can remove any firearms. The word is he has stolen firearms. So this should add more to his jail time.

Today there were two state troopers here. I talked to one of them about all the crime, etc. Going on here. The trooper said they were just checking the area as there has been a lot of burglaries, in the valley. After the trooper left I see that tenant, that was arrested, for beating up his girlfriend, just drove out. We all thought he was in jail. I found out when he came home he had a lot of stolen items. His girlfriend threw him out. Also another tenant, in a family unit, saw him go out with the new tenant and another tenant and came home late at night. So all three may be involved in the valley burglaries. State police were here again and ordered him off the property. He came right back the next day.

The owners rule is any unregistered vehicle will be towed away. Up at the family units there is one car unregistered and a stolen inspection sticker and a wreck. Another tenant's car has no license plates. But they have been sitting up there like that for a long time and nothing has been done.

The tenants in a family unit that have been served an eviction notice. Today the service came to get rid of their bed bugs, for the second time. But they did nothing to get ready for the service and then they left and will come back after they leave and get rid of the bed bugs.

Then three state troopers showed up at the same unit. Brought out the tenant and searched his car. Then left without taking him in. Then the sheriff came to serve papers to another tenant, in a family unit.

Kids have been running around stealing plants, tomatoes etc. from tenants in our area. The property manager was called and he came today. He said he would talk, to the parents, about it but he can't do anything more. That's because he's worthless. He is afraid to really confront these problem tenants.

Here we go again. It's Saturday afternoon and there are two state troopers up at the family units again. They are here for that criminal that has been evicted. There was some kind of a happening between him and a kid. After his girlfriend throw him out he has been sleeping, at the new tenants unit. Also he had a yelling and noisy goingons in the common room with two kids.

Now there's some crazy guy riding all over here on a dirt bike. Up and down the field, over the banks and flipped the bike.

When the property manager was here the other day I asked about he needs to get rid of another tenant, in a family unit. He said that he doesn't have a criminal record. I told him about that guy being arrested twice this summer. By the state police and why he was arrested. The manager new nothing about it. That's because he knows nothing of what goes on here and when he does he does nothing about it.

Well things are looking up today. Two state troopers were here and took that criminal out of the unit. Handcuffed him and frisked his whole body and then they took him away. He's charged with burglary, theft and rape. He's looking at 90 years in prison.

After some tenants have been complaining for two plus years they need their broken or missing storm doors replaced. They finally did new doors on two units. But other units still need replacements.

Now we are having another inspection [federal]. It's just one thing after another. This crap never ends. No matter what happens the owners still won't do anything to make this place better.

A woman in a family unit, with a lot of kids. She gets a large amount of food stamps. She is selling the food stamps. You give he $40.00 and she will let you have $80.00 in food stamps. That's is a federal offence.

Early one morning there was two skunks outside my unit. Two days later you could still smell skunk. So they had to be around the night before. The owners stopped setting traps to catch the skunks.

The woman, in a family unit, that got an eviction. The manager gave her a 30 day extension of her eviction. At that point the owners will move her furniture, etc. to a storage unit.

The only time we see the manager is when he comes once a month to collect rent checks, from the common room drop. With all the things here that need to be replaced or cleaned up. We hardly ever see the maintenance man.

Early am today when I opened my curtain. There was a small skunk eating the bread I threw out, for the birds.

Now the light at my front door and my next door neighbors front door are out. I called in a work order as the maintenance man is not around.

State police were here again. Up at a family unit. This was due to two small kids, belonging to a tenant, broke into another tenants unit. They harmed her kitten and took it with them back to their unit. Then they took off.

Today, at fire light, by my back door area there was a skunk. Not the same one as before. This one had an all white tail and an all white back.

Again this am a skunk by my back door. That makes 4 different skunks around here. You can tell because each one has different markings and size. Owners won't trap than anymore.

A tenant told me that sometime back. One day when the maintenance man came he was drunk. He dropped his pants and mooned her and another tenant. What a jerk.

I put a work order in two weeks ago. The light at my front door and my next door neighbors front door are out. So far it's not been fixed. There usual response. Finally fixed after 3 weeks. Only because I stopped him and got him to replace the bulbs.

Today the state police and the sheriff were here. They are still looking for the 3rd member of that burglary ring. They finally caught the 3rd member and the mastermind of the burglaries.

Owners had a moving van come to move the evicted tenants things to storage. No one told them the unit number or the, of the tenant. Also no one told them the unit is infested with bed bugs. They called the maintenance man and he drove in and saw the moving van and turned around and left. He came back but stayed away from the area. When the property manager came, he left. Then the property manager left and the moving van left. The movers won't take anything out of the unit until the owners give them a written certificate that the bed bugs have been killed. The service came to get rid of the bed bugs.

At 4am today there was some guy walking around the area. Then you see why tenants keep their unit locked up at night. I keep a loaded pistol handy at all times.

One tenant in a family unit is moving out the end of October. She's tired of all these kids outside her front door. The little boy, of the tenant that's being evicted, and a little girl. There was a sexual incident between them. The state police were called and came and they contacted DCF. The tenant with all those kids will be moving up to the unit of the one that's evicted. Because it has 3 bedrooms. Then the kids will be away from our area, we hope.

The maintenance man said that the unit the woman was evicted from, is a total mess. He said you can't believe how destroyed the unit is. Plus the unit was still infested with bed bugs.

So the service had to come back again, to get rid of the bed bugs. I bet the walls are full of the bugs and may travel to other units.

Maintenance left their trailer parked and the kids are jumping all over it and slamming things into the ramp and rocking the whole thing back and forth.

Now the woman, in a family unit, that has all those kids. For the third time she has bed bugs. The service is here to get rid of them.

There's 3 empty family units and no sign of new tenants. The one that was evicted there's no sign of repairing the unit. Maintenance said the unit is a mess.

One of my neighbors, in a handicap senior unit, will be moving out, in a month. Another empty unit.

Here it is mid November and we already have two snow storms and cold weather. Looks like we are going to have a real snowy winter. In the night there was a deer at the bush, in front of my unit, eating.

Saturday afternoon the sheriff was here again. He went to the family unit to that woman that has all those kids.

Sunday am I see all kinds of deer tracks where tenants park. Also all over the area by my back door.

I just learned that a new tenant will be moving into a vacant family unit. A tenant that knows her says she is a low-life with a bunch of kids. That's all we need is more low-life kids to cause trouble here. Again that shows the property manager is worthless. His job is to see to the welfare of the tenants. He has never done it.

Thanksgiving morning, after another snow storm, there are deer tracks everywhere. At 6 am today there was a spike deer eating the bush at the front of my unit. Spikes were a foot tall but even though it is rifle hunting season, spiked deer are not legal. The antler must, at least one, having two points. The next morning there were two small does eating on the same bush. Another am there was one small doe eating on the bush.

Now we are having another big snow storm. Heavy wet snow. This is the 4th snow storm and it is not even winter. Now we have a mild day, with rain. Next day it was back to snow. It's going to be a long winter.

With all this lousy weather I have not been able to go deer hunting. I can't even get into the area that I usually hunt at.

There are so many things on the property that need to be taken care of. But as usual it's not being done. Snow has brought down trees. Limbs and more. Empty units have not been repaired. There has been no ads for the vacant units to rent them. You hardly ever see anyone from the owners on the property. Especially the property manager. We may see him once a month. That is just to pick up rent checks. But they come around when it's time for unit inspections.

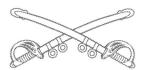

The only smart tenant moved out of here to a senior housing in Utah. She's doing much better then she did here. More healthy and not all the stress from other tenants and the manager, that she had here.

I brought up, to the manager, so many things that need to be done, on the property. His answer they will get to all them, in the spring. As before when spring comes they find an excuse to put it off.

Now we just had our yearly inspection, by the owners. What a joke. The manager never fully checked my stove. The oven control doesn't work. The woman that came said two of the kitchen wall plugs don't work. All I did was push the reset button and they both work. She's so stupid she couldn't even do that. She's a moron. That's the kind of people they hire. Also nobody checked the medicine cabinet, it's rusty. I showed all of this to the maintenance man and I got a new stove and cabinet.

Both the manager and the maintenance man were smoking about 5 feet from the HUD sign that you have to be 25 feet from the building, to smoke. They bitched at tenants but they ignore it themselves. Also the manage exempted the family units from the 25 foot rule in violation of HUD's rules. That's the kind of people the owners are and tenants have to put up with stupid people running the complex.

They tell us now there will be other federal inspections. All the owners are interested in doing is making a show and not what they should do to take care of things needed.

Also there is still three tenants that should be evicted. Two are drug addicts and the other one with 5 kids is selling her food stamps. A federal offense.

The tenant that moved to Utah called me. She said twice the manager sent her security deposit refund and both times it came back. She told him to give it to me to deposit in her bank account. First time it was sent the post office said no such address. The second time he had the wrong zip code. She gets all the mail I send her.

Today up at the family units there was two state police cars and the sheriff's car, domestic violence.

At the yearly inspection the manager finally realized that that drug addict was smoking inside and also marijuana. There rules say that's an eviction. But he's such a coward he only gave him a warning. I told the manager last summer he was smoking inside. He also drives everywhere and has no driver's license.

My neighbor fell on the ice, on the sidewalk because it wasn't taken care of and hurt his back and damaged his cell phone. There answer was to do nothing for him.

The woman that's in charge of rents and other things. She doesn't follow HUD rules and makes up her own rules. When you prove her wrong she has a nasty mouth to tenants.

Today is HUD's rescheduled inspection because of a snow storm. They only went to 3 units, out of 24, and left. I sent a list to the manager what needs to be done here. Also a list to the woman from the housing authority of the poor work that was done at the rehab they financed. No answers from either one.

The owners have hired several new people. We don't know them and they need to have identification that they work for the owners. Every company does this. Without that I won't let them in.

Now the sheriff was here and arrested a wanted person, on the property. There was an arrest warrant out for him.

Well after almost 10 years in public housing. It's time to find a way out of here. To be away from idiots running this complex and incompetent office people. In my time here there's been 5 managers and each one is worse then the one before. The present manager has no clue of how to be a manager. He picks on decent tenants and he's afraid to do anything about the worst tenants. He's been told of trouble makers, drug dealers and more and does nothing about it. The Tenants Association sent him a letter which expressed all this and put him in his place. His answer is not to come here anymore. The owners are in violation of HUD's rules and regulations. HUD has been told about it. Also the State Housing Authority, DCF, along with our senator. No help and there should be a federal investigation for misuse of federal money.

It's time for me to find a better place to live and far away from here.

Well the snow is melting away, from a long snowy winter. The weather is getting better and warmer. So it's back to hearing parents yelling and swearing at their kids. Idiots driving fast through the property. Holes in the roads. The maintenance man sitting in his company van reading the newspaper and smoking. Instead of working. People smoking in violation of HUD's rules and the smell of marijuana.

Good bye!!!!!!!!!!!

Post Script

thought my book was finished. But as more problems arise and incidents. I felt I need to add this last part.

The owners plan to let in a new tenant who they have been told he's a drug dealer, a con man, he has a criminal record and there is an outstanding warrant for his arrest, in another state.

A new tenant in a family unit is conducting a business out of her unit in violation of the owners rules. The tenant with 5 kids just sideswiped another tenants car. Also she's selling her food stamps. A federal offense.

This place won't let me finish my book. A decent tenant has been charged on a trumped up charges. He has not even had a court hearing on the charges. Yet the manager already gave him a hand written eviction notice. The tenant's parole officer told the manager he can't do that. He has not been convicted of anything.

At least there is some good news to end this book. That drug dealer, that was trying to move in, has been denied. His references did not hold up. Bad news the drug dealer appealed the decision and they will let him in. I did a criminal background check on him and came up with 12 criminal charges in this state. I don't know what kind of background check the owners did but they need to learn to do it right. I told the manager what I found. He said they must be old ones he can't use. I said they are not and he's not doing his job.

The saga goes on and on and on.

This is really-----------Good bye!!!!!!!!!!!!!!!!!!!!!!!!!!!!! Yes

Printed in the United States
By Bookmasters